LETHAL IMPACT

Every minute detail shouted at Phillips through his scope. He watched as Young advanced off the porch, moving like a hunter on the trail of a deer. He was obviously dangerous and prepared to fire. Rifle pointed, he walked toward where Gho and Walker stood with their backs against the side of the next house.

Phillips had no choice. A policeman was going to die unless . . .

He centered his crosshairs against the left side of the kid's head next to the ear. While a man shot off-center in the brain may flop about like a dying chicken, a man shot precisely through the brain next to the ear dies immediately.

A clean kill. It reduced the chances of the guy jerking the trigger reflexively during his death throes.

Phillips suspended all emotion. He stroked the trigger gently, squeezed it. The rifle recoiled.

The bullet struck Kevin Young like a charge of electricity. . . .

Books by Charles W. Sasser

Doc: Platoon Medic
  (with Daniel E. Evans Jr.)
Smokejumpers
Last American Heroes
  (with Michael W. Sasser)
Shoot to Kill
Always a Warrior
Homicide!
The 100th Kill
One Shot—One Kill
  (with Craig Roberts)
The Walking Dead
  (with Craig Roberts)

Published by POCKET BOOKS

SHOOT TO KILL

COPS WHO HAVE USED DEADLY FORCE

CHARLES W. SASSER

POCKET BOOKS

New York   London   Toronto   Sydney   Tokyo   Singapore

An *Original* Publication of POCKET BOOKS

POCKET BOOKS, a division of Simon & Schuster Inc.
1230 Avenue of the Americas, New York, NY 10020

ISBN: 0-671-78929-5

First Pocket Books printing July 1994

10 9 8 7 6 5 4 3 2

POCKET and colophon are registered trademarks of Simon & Schuster Inc.

Cover photo © Hans Halberstadt/Arms Communications

Printed in the U.S.A.

This book is dedicated to my friend, partner, and brother police officer, William F. McCracken. It is also dedicated to officers who have given their lives in the line of duty.

Acknowledgments

I should like to give special acknowledgment to the police officers and detectives who so generously shared with me their stories included in this book. Brave in risking their lives in the continuing war against crime, they were equally brave in exposing their hearts and souls to explain an area of police work often shrouded in mystery and fiction. To the policemen who know because they have experienced it, the use of deadly force must always be a last resort. Not only are lives lost, but lives are also inalterably changed and damaged.

In their willingness to face hostile gunfire in the combat zone that is modern America, these men and women in blue represent what may be considered the final defense against the forces of darkness and evil that threaten to bring a once great nation to its knees. They are soldiers in a strange war that will never end.

I should also like to thank my agent, Ethan Ellenberg, who, for these past ten years, has guided my

ACKNOWLEDGMENTS

career as a writer, and who has proved himself a friend as well.

Finally, a note of gratitude to my editors and friends Paul McCarthy and Eric Tobias, who have in numerous ways supported and directed my development as a writer and chronicler of our times.

Author's Note

In this book I have endeavored to render the truth as remembered by the police officers I interviewed. Accordingly, the re-created dialogue and events are their best recollections of what was said and done at the time. Quite naturally, however, one person's interpretation of events will never be exactly the same as another's.

As an ex-police officer myself, a veteran of fourteen years in the streets of Miami, Florida, and Tulsa, Oklahoma, I have acquired some insight into the cop's world and his adaptation to it. I have also had to shoot to kill. I know how the policeman feels when guns start going off. That knowledge and experience, I trust, have lent insight and depth to this chronicle of policemen in combat.

In those chapters that give accounts of my own experiences, I have chosen to tell them in the third person to keep them consistent with the rest of the book.

AUTHOR'S NOTE

The names of most of the police officers, murder victims, convicted suspects still under sentence, and other law enforcement officials, as well as certain others are the real names of actual persons. However, in some instances names have been changed, including the name of one policeman whose honest account of an incident may cause him problems. (Officer Ronald Mallory, chapter 28, is not the actual name of this officer.)

As a rule, I have changed the names of witnesses, crime victims other than those who are dead, suspects who have been released back into society, juvenile offenders, and other people somehow involved in these events for whom public exposure would serve no good purpose.

Contents

Preface   xv

1 Lieutenant David Miles,
  Hallandale, Florida   1

2 Police Firearms Training   11

3 Officer Chuck Sasser,
  Miami, Florida   17

4 Corporal Steve Ecker,
  Sand Springs, Oklahoma   30

5 Detective Sergeant
  George Haralson, Tulsa, Oklahoma   38

6 The Cops' "Old West"
  Mentality   50

CONTENTS

7 Officer Bill McCracken,
Tulsa, Oklahoma   55

8 Officers Mike Little and
Kevin Johnson, Tulsa, Oklahoma   64

9 Gun Control   76

10 Officer Chuck Sasser,
Miami, Florida   83

11 Officer Dennis Johnson,
Tulsa, Oklahoma   94

12 Officer Dallas Williams,
Washington, Pennsylvania   101

13 A "Second Chance":
The Bulletproof Vest   107

14 Officer Stacey Collins,
Littleton, Colorado   115

15 Officer Gene "Buddy" Evans,
Arlington, Texas   121

16 Narc Officer Dwight Stalls II,
Newport News, Virginia   127

17 Special Weapons and Tactics   134

18 Officer Bob Connolly,
Milwaukee, Wisconsin   140

19 Officer Rick Phillips,
Tulsa, Oklahoma   147

20 Officer Chuck Foster,
San Diego, California   157

21 Police Casualties   169

22 Officer Joey Bartlett,
Shreveport, Louisiana   176

23 Police Chief J. B. Hamby,
Catoosa, Oklahoma   185

24 Officer Bernie Swartz,
Pinole, California   191

25 Officer Robert F. Pyles,
Toll Facilities Police, Maryland   202

26 Officer Scott Rakow,
Miami Beach, Florida   208

27 Cop Humor   216

28 Officer Ronald Mallory,
Boston, Massachusetts   218

29 Officer Jay Rapp,
Miami, Florida   221

30 Officer Chuck Sasser,
Tulsa, Oklahoma   227

31 Police Combat Fatigue   233

32 Lieutenant Bill Butler,
Miami, Oklahoma   239

CONTENTS

33 Officer Dwight Stalls II,
Newport News, Virginia 246

34 Detective George Haralson,
Tulsa, Oklahoma 252

Afterword 265

Preface

Although it had been drilled into him at the police academy that cops were often assaulted and sometimes killed on America's mean streets, Police Officer David Freiberger had the attitude of many new rookie cops. He assumed because he wore a uniform and badge he would automatically be respected as a symbol of the law. He never *really* believed anyone would shoot or stab him or try to do him harm.

Less than a year after he graduated from the police academy and took to the streets, he answered a routine disturbance call and stood in front of a screen door. A sixty-eight-year-old ex-convict shot him through the gut without warning.

He survived, but his attitude changed. "It's a war out there," he said.

It *is* a war out there. Each year several thousand American law enforcement officers are assaulted with everything from fists and broken street signs to knives and, of course, guns. A typical year, 1991, saw 130 of them killed in the line of duty.

PREFACE

Police in America were originally patterned after the English version. They enforced the law *unarmed* except for a nightstick and, sometimes, a saber. In the midnineteenth century, however, the men who patrolled tough areas began informally arming themselves against cheap revolvers already being mass-produced in the United States. There was no official action to formally arm policemen until Civil War soldiers began returning with arms and the passion of the war years led to a dramatic surge in violence.

Violence, as today's headlines assure us, has continued to escalate in the United States. There are more than twenty-five thousand homicides annually. Modern criminals arm themselves with sophisticated weapons right up to machine guns. At a time when society grows more sensitive to the rights of individuals and, therefore, to the rights of the criminally accused, lawbreakers have become more calloused and less respectful of the law and citizens' rights.

As recently as twenty years ago police applied the "fleeing felon" rule when it came to the use of deadly force—deadly force being defined as force a police officer may apply in enforcing the law, up to and including the taking of life. Under the "fleeing felon" rule, a police officer could shoot to kill any suspected felon who resisted arrest or attempted to flee.

Today, in most jurisdictions, police can use deadly force under two conditions only: They can shoot in order to protect their own lives, or they can shoot to defend the lives of others. Even then, they had better be prepared to justify their decisions to police shooting boards, the district attorney's office, possibly to a criminal court judge and jury, and almost invariably to a civil lawsuit.

Shoot, or don't shoot? A policeman has only an instant to make up his mind when some gunman bursts out the door of a convenience store wearing a mask, or when he makes a traffic stop and finds himself staring down the muzzle of a stolen .44 magnum. Hesitation may mean death; misjudgment means he could spend his retirement behind bars with real criminals. Lawyers will argue for months and years over whether he did the right thing.

"Still, I'd rather be tried by twelve than carried by six," goes an old police saying.

Yet, in spite of the violent dope-ridden streets of modern America, relatively few cops are ever required to use deadly force. Most cops carry their weapons for twenty years and never even fire them except on the range. When I became a cop in Miami, Florida, my greatest dread was that I might have to use the deadly gun dragging down on my belt. No cop takes lightly the killing of another human being. If he does, he needs to be quickly weeded out.

I remember arriving at a service station where a police sergeant killed a burglar. The burglar had crashed through a plate glass window trying to escape. The sergeant shot him through the heart. Those were the days when police still shot fleeing felons. The burglar lay crumpled on the parking lot amidst a shower of broken glass that, like thousands of diamonds, picked up the sparkle of nearby street lamps. The cop stood silently over the dead man, his gun dangling from his hand. I had never seen a man so pale.

"I'm not God," the sergeant murmured. "I never wanted to play God."

Not long afterward I understood exactly what he meant. I shot and killed a gunman who was trying to kill me. The man's name was Moses. I placed a single .38 slug through his lungs. He sank slowly to his knees while I watched. Then he pitched forward onto his face and died. I remember that he lost one of his shoes.

PREFACE

Circumstances compel several hundred cops in the United States to play God each year and snuff out other persons' lives. Because I have been there myself, I know and understand that terrifying and dramatic moment when life is up for grabs and the cop has no choice but to use deadly force.

I had never wanted to play God either.

This book is a collection of true dramas about policemen and their use of deadly force. Police officers shoot to kill only as a *last resort*. I selected the chapters in this book to show the many dangerous situations in which officers find themselves while enforcing the law, where shoot to kill is an option whether the officer utilized it or not.

This book takes you up that dark flight of stairs to a spaced-out junkie hiding with an automatic pistol; it takes you charging onto the scene of an armed robbery where bandits are slinging lead; it takes you to where policemen live deadly moments venturing into dark and dangerous places. Even Wyatt Earp's gunfight at the OK Corral pales in comparison to today's street cop and his version of *Shoot to Kill*.

SHOOT TO KILL

1

Lieutenant David Miles, Hallandale, Florida

June 16, 1989, 7:00 A.M.

It made for a nice morning, watching the sun rise red and full out over the Atlantic. It flooded the beach in the rare golden sunshine for which Florida is famous. Lieutenant David Miles stood alone in his blue uniform on the beach and watched breezes tug little tufts of white hair onto the crests of waves that followed each other onto the sand in endless sequence. June had been a warm breezy month.

Miles glanced at his watch. Seven A.M. He still had another hour before the Hallandale police department changed shifts.

Miles thought about going home when his shift was over, shedding his blues and pistol belt, and maybe beach bumming it in the sun until his wife came home from work. Life was damned good. Sixteen years on the job, forty-two years old, and sometimes he still felt like a rookie on his first watch.

Police work got in your blood. Cops 'n robbers as a kid, cops 'n robbers as an adult.

"Don't you think there comes a time when you've pushed your luck a little too far?" his wife asked.

She hadn't worried much before, but now she did. Miles started wearing a bulletproof vest underneath his uniform shirt. It was hot and sticky in the tropical air, but his own blood was even hotter and stickier.

Some dude had rabbited after a patrolman stopped his car at three in the morning prowling the warehouse area. Miles was one of the policemen who flushed him out of hiding. They almost ran into each other in the dark at the corner of a building. Miles jabbed the prowler with the end of his flashlight, jabbed him hard in the gut. Instead of striking flesh, the flashlight jarred against something steel solid.

A gun.

The lieutenant dropped his flashlight and grabbed for his holstered pistol. The prowler did the same, his hand snaking up from his waistband filled with a .357 Smith revolver. He pointed it at the policeman. But then he dropped it and ran, disappearing into the darkness.

Later at the police station, detectives examined the stolen gun. "Look at this, Dave. I want to show you something."

The bullet underneath the hammer bore a striker mark.

"That dude pulled the trigger on you," a detective pointed out. "It just didn't go off. You are one lucky cop."

Killed in the line of duty. That was how the citations read of the three policemen friends Miles had lost in his sixteen years under the badge. The citations sounded so sterile, so impersonal. Words could never really describe what happened. They never gave the full impact of how this scruffy animal drew a Saturday night special and drilled one of them in the rib cage just below the armpit.

Killed in the line of duty.

Miles looked at the striker mark on the bullet meant for him and went immediately to the property room and scrounged a used bulletproof vest.

"Honey, the odds are against someone ever shooting at me again," he assured his wife.

But he could tell she was still afraid.

Lieutenant Miles reluctantly turned from his ocean view when the bank alarm call sounded over the radio. He heard Officer Daniel O'Connell take the call. There was some dead air time while the dispatcher waited for a backup.

"I'll take it," Miles volunteered, keying his mike.

Let the other graveyard cars ride on in for on-time shift change. Ninety percent of all alarm calls turned out to be false anyhow. Employees of banks and businesses were always setting off alarms when they arrived for work. Besides, Miles wanted to talk to his friend O'Connell, called "Doc" because of his initials.

He sailed his cruiser across the intercoastal bridge and turned onto Hallandale Beach Boulevard. The clean geometry of the city's high-rise condos sheened pink in the morning light like the insides of conch shells. Hallandale was a retirement city.

The bank was a modern freestanding building facing the boulevard across a huge parking lot landscaped with little plots of hedges and young palms studded into white concrete. An elderly couple in a Lincoln Continental sat at the drive-in teller waiting for the bank to open. Miles gave the couple a disinterested glance as he drifted onto the parking lot. He checked the front of the bank, saw that it appeared secure, then eased around to the rear parking lot as O'Connell announced his arrival.

"I'll be out back with the security guard," Doc radioed.

Miles parked behind Doc's black-and-white. Doc and the security guard were nowhere in sight. Routine. Check on the alarm, turn it off, and then go home. Waiting, the lieutenant unfastened his seat belt and cracked his door open to let in the morning breeze off the sea. He yawned and sat behind the wheel.

Maybe he'd catch a few winks first before heading to the beach. Doc might even want to go with him. They were old friends.

The security guard strolled out of the bank and across the wide sidewalk toward the waiting officer. Miles glanced at him—a medium-size Latino in his thirties wearing a green uniform and a pistol belt. Security company logo on the front of the shirt. A swarthy man, the officer noted, wearing a taut expression.

Miles yawned again. He was all right on the graveyard shift until the sun came up.

The security guard approached the driver's door. He smiled. "Everything's okay, Officer," he said in heavily accented English.

Miles looked around.

"Where's the other policeman?" he asked.

"He is inside, Officer. He will come out soon."

"I'll wait. Everything's not okay as long as one of my police officers is inside the bank."

The security guard hesitated. Then, suddenly, a gun; for the second time that week Miles had a gun thrust at him. He felt like Wile E. Coyote fooled by the Road Runner.

This gun won't misfire! flashed through his thoughts. Instinctively, he turned in his seat to present his newly acquired bulletproof vest to the pistol muzzle. The movement startled the guard, who jumped back.

Seizing the opportunity, the policeman kicked the open car door wide, into the Latino, and launched himself from the car seat. He grabbed for the guard's gun hand, his fingers clamping around the wrist. In an instant, the two men of about equal size and strength locked themselves together in deadly personal combat.

Even as a Marine in Vietnam, Miles had never faced an enemy in hand-to-hand contact. He realized deep in his being, a realization that shot through his veins in iced adrenaline, that he was fighting for his life. Like an animal, he gouged and clawed and struck out with every weapon his body provided. He tried to knee the guy in the balls, he dug his fingers into every available piece of enemy flesh, into every orifice.

Few men ever know the full definition of *savage*.

Somehow, the two uniformed men—the policeman and the bandit disguised as a security guard—remained on their feet. They careened off the hood of Miles's patrol car, bounced back from the trunk of Doc's. Miles locked both hands around the guard's gun wrist and violently whipped the arm back and forth to dislodge the pistol.

The gun received his full concentration.

A second bandit ran out of the bank and clubbed the officer on the head with the butt of another gun. Miles blacked out, dropped hard, dragging the security guard down on top of him. He felt loose chat on the concrete grinding into his back as his senses quickly returned. The bandit's gun was lodged between their struggling bodies.

It went off with a muffled explosion. The muzzle flame scorched cloth and seared skin. The bullet striking Miles's bulletproof vest felt like a giant fist had rammed into his gut.

Dizzy from the fierce blow to his skull, gasping and short of breath from the fight and the gunshot, Miles somehow clawed his Smith & Wesson 9mm semiautomatic from its holster. He shoved the muzzle into flesh and desperately jerked the trigger. The gun went off.

His enemy grunted, but held on.

Miles pulled the trigger again.

The goddamned thing jammed.

He kept pulling the trigger. Nothing. Just the two original gunshots still ringing in his ears.

The goddamned thing was jammed!

And the guy in the green uniform was about to get his gun free for a second shot.

That wasn't his most immediate problem. Miles became aware of a second man bending over him. He felt something tapping him on the forehead. His eyes filled with a black, deep hole the size of a railroad tunnel. The second bandit was attempting to press his gun muzzle against the policeman's forehead to administer the coup de grace.

Killed in the line of duty.

Screaming silently, his brain filled with the sound of his own shrieking, Miles thrashed his head from side to side.

The bandit's gun discharged. For the policeman, it was like a giant M-80 firecracker had gone off between his lips. For a moment he lost sight of the bandits, his vision filled with lights and colors he didn't know existed. He heard nothing for the ringing in his ears.

The side of his face was black with powder burns and blood-spackled from concrete chips kicked up by the bullet, which had jetted into the pavement an inch from his face.

The security guard pinned the policeman to the parking lot while his partner tried again. Miles felt the cold steel muzzle pressed to his forehead between his eyes, felt the pushing as the gunman started his trigger squeeze.

Oh, God . . . Do not go gentle into that good night . . .

He propelled his head off the concrete as high as he could against the gun. At the last instant he flung his head to the side.

Another M-80 exploded between his lips.

The .38-caliber bullet entered an inch below his left eye. It shattered bone and teeth and splattered the bandits with blood. Miles moaned and went limp.

Both bandits jumped up and ran, thinking they had killed the policeman.

Miles struggled back from blackness. He wasn't done in yet. The left side of his face was numb. On his belly now, and in spite of the pain, he looked underneath his police car at the fleeing bandits. His vision was blurred, red-filmed, and the two gunmen became about sixteen. The eight on the left wore green security uniforms, while the eight on the right wore nylon stocking masks pulled down over their heads.

The lieutenant aimed his pistol at the crowd and squeezed the trigger. Still jammed. He worked the slide free just as the gang disappeared around the corner of the bank heading toward the wide parking lot in front—and just as a *third* bandit exited the door of the bank.

The third bandit snapped a shot at the prone policeman, trying his luck at killing a cop who just wouldn't stay down and die. Missing, this bandit fled in a direction opposite his partners. He caught a metro bus on the boulevard and escaped.

Miles never even saw this suspect, did not hear the gunshot. He had tunnel vision focused on the two who had held him down and tried to execute him. He scrambled from the pavement and gave chase, staggering a little from shock and loss of blood.

Carotid artery.

He *knew* he was dying, that he had about three minutes before he bled out and collapsed. He would not go alone into that good night.

At the drive-in teller, the bandits attempted to commandeer the Lincoln Continental, but the old people locked their doors and rolled up their windows. Just before the bandits could blast their way in, a terrible bloody apparition in blue with a gun in its fist lurched around the corner of the bank. Without hesitation it charged straight at the startled criminals, gun blazing.

The bandits screamed. They returned fire, then bolted as the wounded policeman attacked directly into their muzzle flashes, stumbling and popping off rounds.

He would not be stopped.

Lieutenant Miles had one objective in mind: *kill.* He was going to die, but he'd be damned if his killers ever received the chance for forty legal appeals and eventual release on some legal technicality. The goddamned lawyers weren't going to settle this one.

Miles would settle it himself in hot lead and blood. Right now. On this parking lot.

He lumbered and staggered after the bandits, shooting at them with his semiautomatic. They returned his fire shot for shot over their shoulders as they fled toward a blue Mazda sedan parked on the lot near the boulevard. Their getaway car. The security guard had a .38 revolver cracking off rounds from each hand.

Functioning on instinct and training, the lieutenant ran over to a spindly little palm and knelt behind it for cover. He quickly slapped a fresh magazine of ammo into the butt of his 9mm. The tree trunk wasn't three inches in diameter, but it was the nearest thing available.

In the meantime, Doc, who the bandits had earlier taken by surprise and tied up inside the bank, slipped his bonds. The bandit left to guard him had gotten cold feet and abandoned his accomplices when the shooting started outside. That was the third suspect who took a shot at Miles before fleeing to catch a bus.

Doc still had his service pistol. Apparently, the bandits—Nicaraguan immigrants—had never seen a security holster before. They had tugged and jerked at the holstered weapon until Doc could have laughed at their efforts, but they finally gave up and left the pistol where it was.

Hearing the firefight proceed from the back of the bank to the front, O'Connell ran out the front into the bright morning sunlight that bathed the nearly empty parking lot. The first thing he saw was the two robbers running and throwing lead back over their shoulders. In hot pursuit was Lieutenant Miles, drenched in his own blood.

Fear for his friend's life lent speed and accuracy to Doc's shooting. Crouched on the bank steps, he fired his semiautomatic, weak hand supporting strong hand. The policeman pumped rounds methodically at the two-gunned security guard and his stocking masked accomplice. Loaded with a fresh magazine, Miles's big 9mm rejoined the deadly symphony of death.

The bandits reached the Mazda, but that was as far as they got. Back against the car, the security guard made his last stand, both .38s popping. His partner threw himself into the car and onto the floorboard.

The superiority of police firepower in the cross fire shattered every window in the car, sending shards of glass sparkling through the sun laced Florida air. Bullets punctured doors and hood with sharp metallic clangings. Sparks exploded from bullets striking metal. The policemen emptied their weapons. It was a "mad minute," like the times of free fire in Vietnam when Miles was with the Marines.

The security guard's body jerked and danced as lead ripped into his body. He dropped dead to the pavement with nine bullet wounds.

The shooting ceased. An abrupt silence. The second bandit, unscathed but frightened to near shock, had to be pried off the floorboard of the Mazda, like removing a cat from a screen door. Doc had him out on the parking lot facedown and handcuffed by the time backup units began arriving.

Lieutenant Miles staggered up to the dead man and stood over him, looking down. It had almost been *him* dead on the pavement in the morning sun. He started trembling. Less than ten minutes ago he stood watching the sunrise over the Atlantic. How quickly a life changed, how quickly and brutally it could end.

Doc encircled the wounded policeman with his arm to support him.

"It's over, partner," he said. "Dave, we need to get you to a hospital."

Miles blinked. He looked around. The bullet must not have severed his carotid after all.

"I'm going to live," he said.

"Yes."

"I'm really going to live!"

POSTSCRIPT: Lieutenant David Miles medically retired from the Hallandale police department because of irreparable damage inflicted to his senses by the gunshot wound to his face. Police captured the third would-be bank robber in Sweetwater, Florida, about six months later. The two surviving bandits are currently awaiting trial for their crimes.

2

Police Firearms Training

Up until recently, the standard issue sidearm for most police departments was the six-shot .38-caliber Colt or Smith & Wesson revolver with a four-inch barrel. Detectives commonly carried a smaller five-shot version with a two-inch barrel. However, many departments are now seeking heavier firepower in 9mm semiautomatics and even .45s. The narcotics trade with its combination of doper paranoia and lots of dirty money has produced street criminals frequently better armed than most policemen. America's modern outlaw sometimes comes out blazing with semiautomatics and even automatic weapons of his own.

Police arms rooms also contain increasingly sophisticated weapons for special purposes—scoped .270 or 30.06 sniper rifles, shotguns, machine pistols, M16 assault rifles, and even submachine guns. Specially equipped SWAT (Special Weapons and Tactics) or SOT (Special Operations Teams) are prepared to conduct full military assaults against entrenched or barricaded *squads* of criminal gunmen or terrorists.

Policemen say it all the time: "It's a war out there, a *war.*"

While police officers are dissuaded from depending upon weapons as a quick solution to complex street problems, they are taught nonetheless to use them with cold and deadly purpose whenever necessary.

"It's not Hollywood out there," goes a standard spiel in police academies across the nation. "You don't shoot the asshole in the leg, you don't shoot the gun out of his hand, and you don't shoot at tires. You never, *never,* fire warning shots. You draw and fire that gun for one reason and one reason only—to kill the bastard. You aim at the widest part of the target—and you *kill* it. When you're firing out there, you're firing for only one reason: It's *your* life—or it's *his.*"

Most police shootings do not occur against desperate and heavily armed terrorists like California's Symbionese Liberation Army. The majority occur at very short range, suddenly and unexpectedly in some seedy tenement hallway or in a dark back alley. The policeman doesn't have time to think. He merely reacts. Any decisions he makes are based solely upon his survival instincts and his training.

Because of the sudden nature and close proximity of most police gunplay, weapons instructors place heavy emphasis upon quick point shooting during regular in-service firearms qualification and requalification. Police officers are required to qualify on the range at least once a month.

The standard police firearms range consists of three target distances—seven yards, fifteen yards, and twenty-five yards. Policemen fire the traditional strong-hand-supported method from each position.

The firer crouches at the knees to make the smallest possible target and the quickest, steadiest platform for his weapon. He thrusts both hands straight out in front of him, elbows locked, weak hand supporting the gun hand, and squeezes off rounds. Some departments train their officers to cut down on the possibility of bystander injuries by firing no more than two shots at a time before pausing to judge the effect of their gunfire.

From the fifteen and twenty-five yard lines, officers also fire the kneeling and prone and unsupported one-hand-only positions. Finally, using both their left and right hands, they fire around and over barricades meant to simulate the corners of buildings or over the hoods of cars.

Policemen are required to bull's-eye at least thirty shots out of the fifty-shot course. Most shoot better than that.

There is a big difference, however, as some policemen discover, between shooting at a man-target and an actual man who might be shooting back. Even range experts have been known to empty their guns in combat firing at men less than ten feet away without making a single hit. It's easy for even a well-trained policeman to forget every good marksmanship habit he ever learned when the lead starts flying and his adrenaline pumping.

Teaching policemen *how* to shoot is in many respects easier than teaching them *when* to shoot. Individual policemen must make life or death decisions in an instant.

"It's scary," admitted New Orleans police officer Gregory Powell. "There was this kid about twelve or thirteen, a *big* kid but still a kid. We're looking for this suspect in an armed robbery. It was dark and this kid matches the description. I jump out of my cruiser and throw down on him. He turns around—and he's got this gun in his hand.

"What the hell was that kid doing out that time of night anyhow?

"Look, I could have shot him. I could have killed him. I had already put about a pound of pressure on the trigger. The hammer was starting to go back when he dropped the gun. It was a *toy* gun. A toy.

"How was I to know that? Maybe I would have gotten off with excusable homicide, but his parents would have sued me. Because you're a cop people expect you to know the difference between a kid with a toy gun aimed at you and a robber with a real gun.

"But how are you going to know that at night when it happens that fast? Tell me, how are you going to know? It's scary."

The fastest way for a rookie to wash out of a police academy is to demonstrate poor judgment in the use of deadly force. In a society gone wild with civil litigation, with a hungry lawyer waiting in every shadow, cities have become increasingly lawsuit-conscious. Shoot-Don't Shoot courses and pop-up combat courses eliminate scores of police trainees annually. When faced with simulated real-life situations during which they must make deadly force decisions, cadets who consistently "shoot" butchers and little old ladies with umbrellas are looked upon with suspicion and likely dropped from training.

One police candidate was placed into a test situation in which a knife wielding officer playing the part of the "bad guy" held a female hostage in front of him. The candidate was armed with an unloaded service revolver.

"What would you do?" he was asked.

The candidate was a young veteran of the 82nd Airborne Division. He lifted his pistol and took careful aim.

"Let her go or you're dead meat," he said.

The bad guy refused. The candidate "shot" him

between the eyes. Although veteran officers may have taken this same action, the candidate was denied admittance to the police department. The reasoning was that he had been too willing to resort to deadly force, not that he was necessarily wrong. A rookie who could "kill" like that even before he took to the streets, so the reasoning went, might be too eager to use force in a real-life crisis.

There are indeed officers on every police department known to their comrades as being a little "gun happy" or heavy-handed. Some of them even carry "throw downs," unregistered, untraceable weapons that may be placed on a dead suspect's body in the event they make a mistake. The story is told of a Miami, Florida, policeman who cornered a known thief, rapist, and all-around bad guy in a dark back alley. The character resisted arrest. The policeman shot and killed him, thinking he had a weapon.

The dead man turned out to have been unarmed. But when homicide detectives and a shooting team arrived to investigate, they turned the body over and discovered something like two guns and six knives underneath it. Every officer on the scene had secretly slipped a throw down underneath the corpse to protect a fellow cop.

Although few cops actually carry throw downs, it is not unusual for a policeman to carry a backup or "hide" gun. Especially when he works a busy district he perceives as being exceptionally dangerous.

For years working Miami's Liberty City and Overtown ghettos, Officer Chuck Sasser carried a tiny two-shot .357 magnum derringer as a backup gun. He had grown wary after having been stabbed once, shot at several times, and assaulted too many times to count. Most ghetto cops carried more than one gun.

Whenever he made a car stop that warranted caution, he palmed the derringer and kept it ready. If the motorist was legit, he never even knew the policeman had a gun in his hand.

One night Sasser stopped a low-rider Buick jammed with dudes all as scroungy and mean-looking as skid row hookers. Unknown to him at the time, the wild bunch had just stuck up a convenience store. The slicks in the backseat shuffled around to hide their guns as the officer walked up to them. They were probably waiting to see what he did before deciding on whether or not to knock off a nosy cop. The driver gave the policeman a truly evil grin.

As soon as Sasser read the situation, he knew he would die trying to reach <u>his holstered</u> service revolver. But he had the derringer in his left hand. With a casual flick of the wrist, he cocked the miniature gun and shoved it up to ADD OIL in the driver's ear, took up what little trigger slack there was, and grinned back at the carload.

"Just one asshole moves and I'm gonna put this dude's brains in your laps," he promised, bluffing but not bluffing.

It worked. The scum bags dropped their guns and ended up in jail. Sasser ended up staying alive.

For the cop, that's the game—staying alive.

3

Officer Chuck Sasser,
Miami, Florida

1965–68

The thing that bothered Sasser most when he first
became a cop was that he might have to shoot and kill
somebody. Training Officer McFann lined up all the
rookies in front of the police academy in Miami. As
they filed by him, he made them sign their names
before Big John the armorer issued each of them a
revolver. Sasser's was a chrome-plated .38 Smith &
Wesson. He had handled guns all his life, having
started hunting squirrels in the hills of Oklahoma
when he was eight years old, but the purpose for which
he was given *this* gun made it seem heavy and
awkward. He stood there staring at it in his hands. It
dawned on him that this thing of fighting crime was
for *real*.

Officer McFann grinned. "That weapon is your
brother, your sister, your wife, and your savior," he
said. "Treat it with respect. It will save your life when
nothing else can."

Sasser wasn't sure, when it came right down to it, if
he could save his own life if it meant icing someone

17

else. Although he found out later that the other rookies had the same kind of doubts, none of them let on. The police is a macho world. A cop is not supposed to show weaknesses and doubt—ever.

"You have to be able to go to hell itself and make a collar," Officer McFann said. "You have to show the devil that you have more guts than he has."

McFann was tough and he wanted his rookies to be tough. He was so *strike* the rookie cadets figured he starched his underwear and chewed razor blades. He didn't even sweat when he climbed into the Bear Pit for "dirty fighting." Officer McFann would have made a great Marine DI; maybe he had been one. He personally saw to it that, as long as he was at the Miami police academy, no wimps, sissies, or anyone who so much as took a whiff of quiche ever pinned on a Miami police badge. That was before the recent era of women in patrol cars.

"Gil de Rubio!" he bellowed into the face of a cadet standing rigidly at attention. His jaw jutted and his ice blue eyes froze the cadet in his shoes. "What's a cow, Gil de Rubio?"

The response was ritualistic: "Sir, a cow is a four-legged, lactating mammal of the bovine species with . . ."

If the response was one word off, or if the cadet hesitated one beat too long, or if he didn't belt it out, then he went down for push-ups. Or he ran a mile. Or he went through the confidence course. Or, worse yet, he got into the Bear Pit to fight all 240 pounds of romping, stomping, Nebraska-fed Cuddles.

"Don't be a wimp. He's just a rookie too. Get in there and *get* him."

If the offender survived Cuddles, he had to run some more or stand at attention in his little khaki uniform.

"I don't want to see one eyeball click, you understand, rook? Indecision can get you killed. I don't care if my rookies are shot by jealous husbands or die of heart attacks, but you're not going to be killed in the streets because that would reflect on me. Do you understand? I am going to make a man out of you. A police*man*. A police*man* is tough. A police*man* is at war. In the streets you are *The Man.*"

The guns issued by Officer McFann quickly became a part of the rookies. They carried them so much they felt undressed without them. They practiced constantly on the range. It was an indoor range with target lanes where man-outline targets moved up and down the lanes toward and away from the shooters. Most police combat shooting, the new policemen learned, occurred at about seven yards or less. That meant a policeman was looking the perp eyeball to eyeball when he shot him.

Or the perp shot the cop.

"You want your first shot to hit him," Officer McFann said. "One shot may be all you get. It's point snap shooting. Point for the widest part. That's the chest. Drill him through the heart and he's gone. He'll keel right over and lie still. Shoot a scum bag in the head and sometimes he flops around a lot."

He fixed the rookies with his gaze.

"Don't hesitate to shoot if you have to," he said. "But make sure it's necessary to shoot. You'll have to live with it the rest of your life—or you may find yourself charged with murder the same as anyone else."

The rookies looked at each other.

"How can we be sure it's necessary?" somebody asked.

"There are three times you are authorized by law to use deadly force," McFann said. "You can shoot a

19

fleeing felon, you can shoot in self-defense, or you can shoot to save someone else's life. Does that answer your question?"

"Yes, sir."

It didn't. When the time came, *if* it came, how did a cop know *for sure?*

"You're going to be expected to make split-second decisions out there in the streets. It'll take courts months or years to decide if you were right or not," the training officer said.

It was all a little scary.

"What do you think?" Cadet Albert Harrison asked Cadet Sasser. "Think you can shoot somebody that needs shooting?"

Sasser hesitated. "Do you?"

"I can shoot him," Harrison said.

"Me, too," Sasser said.

He looked away. He hoped it never came to that.

But then he was assigned to work the toughest district in the city. It was a combination of skid row and ghetto. In a city with the highest crime rate in the nation, he worked a district with the highest rate of violence in the city. If he was ever going to have to shoot someone, then *The Zoo,* which is what cops called the beat, was probably where it would happen.

His first experiences almost overwhelmed him. Every night it was junkies and prostitutes and family fights and shootings and stabbings. They were mean streets. Sasser didn't simply *perceive* the cop's world as dangerous and hostile, as sociologists liked to put it; the cop's world *was* dangerous and hostile.

"It's a war out there in them streets," Officer Vic Butler used to say. Butler was tough, like McFann. Everyone said he had killed three men during his twenty years in the streets.

Radical militants lured Butler to a Liberty City project and gunned him down. There were seventeen bullet holes in his body when the EMTs lugged it off. The police never found his killers.

A cop had to be tough to work The Zoo. Otherwise, the street garbage chewed him up and spat out the bones. The new rookies were young enough and reckless enough to believe they could do it all. They had their pistols and shotguns and clubs and a dose of macho. Sasser didn't even notice when a certain tautness around his eyes narrowed them.

Life took on a different perspective. The cop saw a side of human nature that few other people saw regularly if at all—that few would want to see. It changed a policeman's attitude toward society and toward the people who populated it. His outlook narrowed and hardened. The gun he wore on his side was no longer the burden it seemed at the beginning. He no longer seemed as reluctant to use it if the need arose.

Sasser was changing. The streets were changing him.

Every night, what he saw and experienced changed him a little more.

Each Friday night, as regular as midnight, a common-law couple got drunk and cut each other with knives. One night, the female caught the male asleep. She took out a butcher knife and skillfully whacked off his penis. He bled to death before the ambulance arrived.

Tanya the hooker had a pimp who used wire clothes hangers to tie her to the bed as punishment for holding out trick money on him. She got gangrene and lost her right leg at midthigh. She didn't know any other trade, so she still took to the streets. She stood on her favorite corner in skintight shorts, balanced on her crutches, with the stub of her leg rising and falling with her expectations.

"Hey, dude, wanna good time?" Crooning her litany. "Dude, dude? Wanna good time?"

A street gang stabbed a Puerto Rican one hundred times because he unwittingly took a shortcut across the Baby Browns' turf. Young junkies OD'd on heroin in some musty condemned building where cops had to kick the rats off the corpses. Ten-year-olds stole cars and snatched purses and shot twelve-year-olds with live ammo. Kids ran as wild as little animals; girls thirteen-years old gave birth in order to draw welfare, and everybody on the streets despised the cop because he was *The Man*. Mean dudes in porkpie hats and skinny legged trousers and platform shoes clutched themselves in belligerent groups on the streets, dealing dope, and shouting, "Oink! Sooo-eee, pig!" when the police went by.

It disillusioned rookies to discover that everything wasn't always nice and legal and by the book. They learned to stretch the law or to ignore it, or they made up their own law as they went along. Petty crimes like burglary and larceny and most shootings and stabbings in which no one died were so common that cops often didn't even bother to make reports on them. Even if they made reports and an arrest, the courts were so overcrowded that the majority of cases were either dismissed or plea-bargained down to misdemeanors and the perpetrators were back out on the streets the next day laughing about it.

Cops involved in minor shootings in which they shot but didn't kill someone sometimes didn't even bother to make reports on it. Cops and bad guys accepted their lumps and gave lumps back because everybody thought that was the way it was supposed to be.

It was a war in The Zoo and the war raged with no holds barred. Vic Butler wasn't the only casualty.

Officer John Olin got shot in the back. He took a

lunch break at an open-fronted cafe downtown; some freak slipped up behind him, grabbed the officer's own gun from his holster, and shot him with it. Sasser always sat with his back against a wall after that.

A twenty-one-year-old rookie answered a trouble call to the Sir Prince Hotel where militants ambushed him. They drilled the rook through the skull with a high-powered rifle.

Motorcycle traffic officer Ron McLeod pursued an escaping armed robber. They came face-to-face with each other at a street corner. The dirt bag shot McLeod off his motorcycle, shot him point-blank in the face. McLeod had three small children.

Like Officer McFann said, in a war a cop had to be prepared to shoot somebody. It always annoyed Sasser to hear some joker retiring from a major police department make the comment that he never even had to *draw* his gun during twenty years' service, as though that were both something he should be proud of and an indictment of any other cop who did. Sasser always figured the reason the cop never had to draw his gun was because he was working a school guard crossing or getting a broad ass holding down a desk at a precinct. Big city cops working the streets for twenty years, if they did a job, were going to at least *draw* their guns.

The first time Sasser got shot at, his hands trembled so badly afterward he couldn't even drive back to the station house.

A man robbed a convenience store near the Miami River and fled in a black Plymouth. Albert Harrison, riding the beat adjoining Sasser's, jumped up the suspect on Seventh Avenue. That started the chase. The Plymouth took to the expressway at Twenty-first Street and headed north with Harrison two car lengths behind him. Sasser was another car length behind his beat partner.

They pegged speeds at 100 mph. Harrison and Sasser were running fender to fender. Sasser glimpsed Harrison intently fighting the wheel. It was late enough in the evening that traffic was light.

The first *pop* surprised both policemen. They instinctively veered their cars. At *that* speed, the suspect was shooting at them! They heard the gun popping again and again and saw muzzle flashes. They found out later most of the suspect's bullets were hitting the rear window post of his own vehicle. They couldn't tell at the speed they were traveling whether the bullets were striking their cars or not. So far, the windshields hadn't spider-webbed.

The suspect lost control of his Plymouth on a cloverleaf near Liberty City. The car sent washes of sparks flying as it scraped the guardrails, banging off either side in the curve. Then it swapped ends a couple of times. Sasser locked brakes and almost slid into Harrison, who had also locked his brakes.

Abandoning his stalled car so quickly that it was still in motion when he jumped out, the robber hurled his empty gun at Harrison's car as the police vehicles barreled down on top of him. Then he surprised the policemen again. He was so desperate to escape that he didn't even hesitate as he sailed off the high cloverleaf overpass to the next level thirty feet below.

Behind him, his car door hung open. Breezes off the ocean caught the loot he left in a torn sack on the seat and turned the money into a green whirlwind. Cash swirled and eddied onto the traffic below. Motorists scrambled out of their cars and started chasing it.

But the bandit's luck had run out. The fall onto the grassy slope next to the other highway below fractured his ankle and knocked the wind from him. What he saw when he managed to look up were two cops leaning out over the higher guardrail with a pair of big revolvers leveled at him.

"Dude, just how much faster are you than a speeding bullet?" Harrison taunted.

Sasser's hands started to shake, now that the excitement was over. That was when he came to the realization that he *could* drop the hammer on a man.

"I'd have shot his eyes out," Harrison said. "I *wanted* to shoot the sonofabitch for shooting at me."

"Yes," Sasser said.

He understood. It was to happen again.

It started with a disturbance call to one of those run-down two-story houses converted to a rooms-for-let. The house was weathered gray; it looked like kids with no plan in mind had constructed it of old building blocks. The door hung open on the side. In the dark, Sasser and his partner Daniels walked down between the house and the side of a pool hall with a dirt floor. Jitterbugs hung around out back drinking wine and smoking dope.

"Looky, looky. It's de *Man*. I be smellin' *pork*."

A garbage can overflowed onto the side porch. Rats scurried out of the way. The policemen stepped inside to a foyer at the bottom of a rickety staircase where a yellow light bulb shone at the end of a long wire hanging from the ceiling. Two men were shouting at each other on the landing at the top of the staircase.

Everything happened suddenly, as it does at such times.

One of the men, for no apparent reason, jerked out a .25 automatic pistol. Instead of shooting the other man, he whirled and pinned Daniels and Sasser to the staircase with four or five quick shots thrown directly at them. *Pop! Pop! Pop! Pop!* Like that.

The second man fell to the floor and started screaming that he was unarmed and giving himself up to the police. The gunman turned and ran down a dark hallway. A door slammed.

He was probably a spaced-out junkie.

Although the stairway was hardly wide enough for one, both Daniels and Sasser lay side by side on their bellies. Sasser's face was directly in front of Daniels's. By now his nerves had steeled to the point that he could even crack a joke at what the uninitiated might term an inappropriate time.

"I can't get any lower," he whispered to his partner, parodying an old World War II *Willie & Joe* cartoon by Bill Mauldin. "Me buttons are in the way."

Cops were good at that kind of black humor. It helped break the tension. Daniels and Sasser lay there like fools snickering and blubbering in each other's face. They had just been shot at, at almost point-blank range, and there they lay, on their bellies in the rat dirt without a scratch on them, snickering at each other.

In the meantime, the assailant holed up in one of the rooms. Every few seconds he cracked his door and hurled another shot down the hallway.

A few years later they might have backed off and called in the SWAT team and negotiators and made a big production of it. But in this tough district, they were accustomed to handling things themselves. This kind of stuff was almost routine in The Zoo. It was the way it was supposed to be. No big deal. You took your lumps and gave lumps back.

Daniels and Sasser waited until the shooter fired a round and slammed the door. They looked at each other and nodded. They jumped up and charged. Daniels had thought to bring his pump shotgun.

They had almost reached the door when it flew open a crack. Out thrust a hand gripping a pistol pointed directly at Sasser's chest. Looking down its muzzle was like peering down a train tunnel.

Sasser thought the train was going to come roaring out of that tunnel and right through his chest. He thought he felt his heart stop beating.

A miracle. The gun did not go off. It vanished and the door slammed.

In that same instant, Daniels blasted a hole the size of a man's head through the door with his shotgun. Although Sasser was still numb from shock, the S&W .38 in his fist remained as steady as if he were sitting down to breakfast. He flattened himself to one side of the door while Daniels took the other side.

Daniels emitted a single curse. The shotgun blast had been like setting off dynamite in an enclosed space. Plaster dust like fine snow sifted from the ceiling. It made ghosts of the policemen. Daniels laughed silently, looking at Sasser.

Sasser wasn't laughing.

Someone inside the room was screaming. It was a woman.

"Po-lice?" came the gunman's voice, frightened now. "Po-lice, I ain't gonna shoot no more."

"You are dead!" Sasser yelled at him. *"Man, you are dead."*

"No! No! Listen—"

"You listen!" Daniels shouted. "Throw out that gun."

"You'll kill me."

"We'll kill you if you don't," Sasser shouted back.

The woman kept screaming. If everyone within five square blocks hadn't heard the shooting, then they surely heard the screaming. It sounded like she was dying.

"I'm giving up," the shooter screeched. "Don't shoot no more, Officers. Don't you shoot no more, hear?"

The gunman's hand ventured hesitantly through the hole in the door made by Daniels's shotgun blast. Two fingers held the semiautomatic pistol. The gun dropped into the hallway between the policemen.

Sasser sprang off the wall and stiff-legged the flimsy door into the gunman's face. An instant later the officers had the man facedown and handcuffed.

The woman was still screaming. The policemen looked at each other in astonishment. She was bucknaked. She resembled a skinny blackbird. She jumped up and down in the middle of the bed clutching her foot with both hands while blood sprayed from it. The best the policemen figured, she had been laid up in bed drunk with her feet propped up on the bed toward the door when Daniels fired his shotgun.

"You muthafuckas!" she shrieked, adding to the image of an angry, naked bird. "Muthafuckas! You done shot off my muthafuckin' little toe."

Afterward, when Sasser thought about it, he remembered Officer McFann's words from the police academy: *Don't hesitate to shoot if you have to.*

He broke into a cold sweat and kept seeing that door open and the gun thrusting out toward his heart. Why had he not reacted instinctively and shot the gunman? Why had he hesitated? Did he still possess inhibitions against shooting a man, even if it meant saving his own life?

One shot may be all you'll get.

It was only a couple of months after the incident with the woman's toe that the team of Daniels and Sasser received a trouble call on a shooting in a bar. The victim lay on the floor kicking his legs and spilling blood while a crowd gathered to watch. The suspect ran out the back door when the police burst through the front door. Daniels paused to take a look at the victim while Sasser chased the gunman down an alley behind a row of housing projects.

It was dark. Few lights shone from windows. Sasser heard the guy ahead slipping and sliding on pork gristle and rotted chili and soured cream and the like.

The tenants dumped their garbage in the alley. It smelled like a pigsty or a slaughterhouse.

Sasser chased the suspect for two or three blocks. They approached the construction site of the new Overtown Expressway. Lights on the site silhouetted the fugitive. The cop was gaining on him. The suspect turned to rip off a shot.

The policeman didn't even think about the garbage. He dived face first into the mess that had already gummed up his shoes. He got off a shot of his own while still in midair.

The guy screamed, but he turned and kept going. Sasser saw him drop in the weeds at the construction site. He knew he had got him.

The only thing that surprised him was *where* he got him. The bullet tore off the man's top lip. No teeth. Just lip. With Daniels's toe and now Sasser's lip, the other cops started making bets on which part of the anatomy they'd get next. Sasser laughed about it as hard as anyone.

His hands weren't even shaking. True, he had shot a man, but he hadn't killed him. That came later. Still, he had changed during the few years on the streets. He was no longer the rookie worried about having to shoot someone.

"Don't worry," he told his wife. "When it comes to getting hurt out there and it's either him or me, then it's going to be *him*."

4

Corporal Steve Ecker, Sand Springs, Oklahoma

December 23, 1982, 7:35 P.M

Sand Springs, Oklahoma, a Tulsa suburb of about sixty thousand people crooked into a bend of the Arkansas River, decorated itself for Christmas and then waited for snow. Two more days. A city councilman on his way home from work stopped at the Family Market off Charles Page Boulevard to pick up a few more things for Christmas dinner. The sun was setting to cap off a pleasant day as he sauntered past the market's wide windows overlooking the parking lot.

Flyers in the window advertised Dove and Tide and Bacon-2 lbs $2.49. The councilman cast a casual glance inside, past the flyers. Shocked by what he saw—someone else also shopping, *with a gun*—he looked around and spotted a pay telephone attached to the outside of the building near the glass doors.

At Sand Springs police headquarters, Corporal Steve Ecker was booking a shoplifter when the dispatcher's head popped out the door of the radio room.

"Armed robbery in progress," she cried. "Family Market."

After dialing the police, the councilman left the phone off the hook and ran. Ecker heard the spiteful *crack! crack!* of twin gunshots erupting from the dispatcher's radio console. Apparently the robber at the Family Market meant business.

Later, witnesses described how the ski masked bandit exploded into the market with a sawed-off shotgun in one hand and a .357-caliber revolver in the other. He appeared hyped-up on crack or something; wide, walling eyes burned through the slits of his red-and-blue ski mask. He blasted one hole in the ceiling with his shotgun, then followed up with two more shots from the revolver. That attracted the attention of holiday shoppers.

"This is a fuckin' robbery!" he thundered. "Don't nobody do nothin'. Or you is dead meat. You motherfuckers hear?"

Adrenaline already pumping from hearing the gunshots, Corporal Ecker ran out of the police station, collecting Officer Mike Chappel on the way. While Chappel drove, speeding toward the armed robbery in progress, Ecker barked commands into the car's radio mike. Although thirty-two-year-old Ecker was only a corporal with three years' police experience, his service with the famed U.S. Army Green Berets had equipped him with the maturity and judgment to be appointed evening shift supervisor for his fifty-two man department.

He had a total of six police patrol cars on duty. He ordered Family Market sealed off—two units at the back, two in front. The other two were out of service on other trouble calls.

"Advise all units," he instructed, "to stay out of sight until the suspect leaves the store."

The market would be crowded with shoppers; the

last thing Ecker wanted was innocent people caught in a crossfire. Or a hostage situation.

In the excitement of organizing the assault, Ecker overlooked his own less experienced partner. Before the corporal had time to react, Chappel careened the police cruiser onto the market's parking lot and braked directly in front of the glass doors.

"Oh, *shit!*"

The bandit had surely spotted them. They had to go for it.

Spilling out of the vehicle, the officers entered the store through the automatic-opening glass doors. Crouching, weapons drawn, tight and tense as the strings of a cheap guitar, Ecker peeled off to the right and went down next to a stack of soft drink crates. Chappel sought cover near the shopping carts.

Ecker's first glance fastened on the slender bandit at the checkout counters. The brightly colored ski mask burned itself into his vision. A masked man, especially if he was heavily armed, always appeared more threatening, almost larger than life.

The bandit had myopic vision. Surprisingly enough, he seemed so preoccupied with his task that he hadn't even noticed the patrol car outside the glass doors or the two blue-uniformed policemen advancing on him. In the crook of his right arm, the hand of which grasped the sawed-off shotgun, he held one of the store sackers hostage——a young blond boy. The muzzle of the big pistol in the bandit's left hand pressed hard against the kid's temple.

The boy's eyes were the size of the special-offer dinner plates on sale at the head of one of the aisles.

"Bring it here! Bring it here!" the bandit chanted, yelling at the cashiers to produce money.

He grabbed cash from the wide-eyed checkers with his pistol hand and stuffed it into his pockets. His elbow crooked tighter around the sacker's throat.

"Move it, you motherfuckers! *Move!*"

On one knee, Ecker thrust his .41-caliber magnum revolver out in a two-handed combat stance.

"Freeze, asshole!"

That wasn't what he meant to say, but that was how it came out. Customers knew exactly whom he was addressing. About thirty of them saw what was coming and hit the floor behind the long row of checkouts, leaving a clear field of fire for the policemen thirty feet away.

Everything was happening so rapidly that Ecker wasn't quite sure what he expected—maybe a stand-off, a "let me go or I'll shoot the kid." But to his surprise and relief, the bandit let go of his senses and, instead of holding onto his hostage, sent the kid reeling and sprawling across the floor with a tremendous shove.

At the same time the gunman pivoted to face the policemen.

His revolver spat flame, cracking loudly within the store's confines. It cracked again.

A woman customer screamed.

Ecker squeezed off five return shots rapid-fire.

Bullets tore into a magazine rack against the far wall behind the robber. The bandit's body jerked. He fell to one knee. But then he jumped up and, leaping and running through customers scattered prone or kneeling on the floor, disappeared down the canned goods aisle toward the back door.

Ecker couldn't believe he had missed all five shots. Breathing hard, panting like after a quarter-mile dash, he crabbed along the front of the checkout.

"Mike, get those people outa here!" he shouted as he started grabbing customers and hustling them toward the front door. It didn't require much urging.

In the meantime, the bandit tried the back door and

found it locked. His only escape lay in shooting his way past the policemen.

The store was now empty except for the policemen and, somewhere inside the half-acre store, the masked man with his two firearms.

Silence.

Ecker took deep breaths and dashed to the head of the canned goods aisle. He crouched next to a rack displaying Zinger cakes and pastries. Chappel found cover in cereals three aisles down. The policemen listened, their eyes darting.

At least seven shots had been fired in the first exchange—and it wasn't over yet. The thing about being a policeman was that you had to finish the job. Everyone else could step back and watch the action and comment on it from the next day's headlines. But the policemen—they were trapped inside the tiger's cage because it was their job to stay there and take care of the tiger. Whatever that called for.

Ecker took advantage of the respite to reload. Empty cartridge casings clattered loudly to the floor in the silence.

He wished he had thought to bring a shotgun.

He took a deep breath.

Chappel's shout froze the breath in his lungs: *"Steve, he's behind you!"*

Instinct, training, *something* took over. It saved his life. Just as he tucked and rolled into the shopping aisle to his left, the Zinger display rack next to where he had knelt exploded. Gunfire splattered cakes and icing for thirty feet around.

Chappel returned fire. Ecker heard three or four more gunshots as he scrambled on his belly for cover. Burned cordite stung his nostrils. Excitement pounded his heart against his ribs.

"I'm hit."

It was Chappel. Fear and dread edged his voice with raw ice.

Ecker lay in the aisle. The bandit was nowhere in sight, but the corporal spotted Chappel pressed hard against the back side of a Coke machine. There was a bullet hole in the machine.

"Where are you hit?" Ecker demanded.

Chappel pointed to his chest protected by a bullet-proof vest.

"Are you hurt bad?"

"I don't think so. But I think I hit the bastard."

"Cover me if you can."

More silence while the combatants caught a few breaths.

Ecker looked around, desperately trying to come up with a better plan than exposing himself once again to potentially lethal gunfire. Bullets had sought his life twice over a period of less than three minutes. You never wanted to push Lady Luck too far; she could be a treacherous bitch.

Sweat formed rivulets on the officer's face.

Funny, he thought. As a kid he had worked sacking groceries and stocking shelves at this same Family Market. Funny how life often made full circles. Now, he thought, life might well close its circle on him within the next few minutes. He calmly accepted that he might never walk out of this store. And with that acceptance came a surge of anger.

His eyes darted. He nodded to himself. Even a lousy plan was better than no plan at all. Once again as he swung into action adrenaline compressed time, forcing all life before and after into this one single point of time.

Silently, gun in hand, Ecker climbed shelf by shelf to the top of the nearest aisle display. Carefully, pushing aside one box of cereal or soap or something at a time, he cleared a gun port view into that section of the store where low freezers contained ice cream, frozen pies, and vegetables, and other similar commodities.

He spotted the bandit hiding behind the freezer nearest the front of the store. The robber had removed his mask to reveal a young black face covered with blood. Ecker drew careful bead on the top of the gunman's head. He took up trigger slack.

The bandit shifted, leaving as target only the back of his head.

Ecker relaxed. Waiting. He wanted to end it with the next shot.

One shot—one kill.

As he waited, he noticed blood smeared all over the floor next to the freezer. Officers later discovered that two of Ecker's first bullets found flesh. One ripped muscles from the calf of the bandit's right leg. The second, amazingly enough for a handgun as powerful as the .41 magnum, caught the robber in the center of his forehead but failed to penetrate the skull. The bullet fragmented and followed the skull around underneath the skin.

During the second exchange of gunfire, Officer Chappel added to the gunman's grief by shattering his right elbow.

It was a badly wounded and bleeding thief whose life would expire as soon as he revealed himself again.

For some odd reason, Ecker recalled the old tale about Sergeant York's yelling *"Gobble! Gobble!"* to induce German soldiers to expose themselves. He was about to use the trick himself when the hiding bandit suddenly shouted, "Okay, okay. I give up."

He tossed his shotgun and pistol into the aisle. A number of spectators outside the store with their noses pressed against the glass watched the bandit slowly stand up with his hands in the air. Ecker took a deep sigh. He was going to see Christmas after all.

So was the bandit.

POSTSCRIPT: Wendell Grayson, twenty-three, had been paroled only thirty days previously from the last of six armed robbery convictions during which he pistol-whipped his victims. He was high on marijuana and PCP when he burst into the Family Market to continue his violent life of crime. He survived his wounds to receive sentences totalling 250 years in the state penitentiary. He will probably be paroled again within five years.

Officer Mike Chappel suffered a nasty bruise from the gunshot he caught to the center of his bulletproof vest.

5

Detective Sergeant George Haralson, Tulsa, Oklahoma

August 29, 1989, 7:40 P.M.

Detective George Haralson didn't realize how sick some people could be until he transferred to SID (Special Investigations Division). Officers in SID worked undercover in narcotics, vice, and underworld intelligence. Sergeant Charley Bush came up to him the first day.

"George, I want you to make a child porn case. I want you to work pedophiles."

A pedophile was an adult sexually attracted to children, but Haralson hardly knew what child porn was. A day ago he was in uniform, the dark green of the Tulsa police department. Uniformed cops rarely came across kiddie porn.

Sergeant Bush handed a photograph to the new plainclothesman. Haralson took one look and recoiled from it in disgust. It showed the face of a little girl of about five or six. She had her eyes squinted and was trying to turn away from a man's penis ejaculating in her face. Obviously, somebody off-camera was holding her.

"That," said Bush, "is kiddie porn."

Within the next few years, Haralson became the acknowledged national expert on child pornography. A federal prosecutor commended him for making more child pornography cases than any other law enforcement officer in the United States. He successfully infiltrated national pedophile organizations such as "The Childhood Sensuality Circle" in San Diego and "The Lewis Carroll Collector's Guild" in Chicago through which the bizarre subculture of the pedophile distributed child erotica. He set up national "sting" operations to trap producers and distributors.

No one ever took him for a cop while he was undercover. Short and stocky with hair thinning on top and straggling down the back of his collar, wearing a Fu Manchu or a mangy mustache and beard, he possessed a round face as pliable and expressive as that of any Hollywood character actor. The face and the shrewd intelligence that accompanied it were George Haralson's gift. With them he became *Everyman, Anyman*—a wino on the street, a petty hustler, a pimp, a doper. In his guise as a connoisseur of children's porn, he became the child pornographer's worst nightmare.

"If you have a hidden camera that takes a photograph of a masked man robbing a convenience store," he liked to say, lecturing other police officers-in-training on the art and science of nabbing pedophiles, "what you have is a photo of a crime in progress. If you have a photo of a nine-year-old girl having sex with a man, you also have a picture of a crime in progress. The type of person who would take a kid as young as five or six and rape and sodomize him or her for the pleasure of others to see in a photograph or movie is a sick and dangerous individual. *That's* the crime of kiddie porn."

When it came to pornography, *anything* went. The freaks were often not satiated by a steady diet of conventional obscenity and reached to baser depths. *Snuff* films show actual sex murders of female victims. Bestiality, sadomasochism . . . Haralson seized photos of a barmaid's seven-year-old son engaged in sexual acts with a Pekingese, of a one-year-old baby being sodomized.

A dirty world. It was a filthy world. Haralson bought a house to which he fled off-duty. He locked all the doors and sat inside the house trying to feel clean again.

Early in his career undercover, Haralson busted forty-two-year-old Thomas Otis Glidewell for taking lewd and obscene photos of his nine-year-old neighbor and peddling them through the pedophile subculture. Glidewell took the stand in his own defense and explained to a jury that his little girl victim was "promiscuous." *She* seduced *him.* The jury's collective mouth dropped open. Glidewell found himself sailing off to prison.

He went through counseling and psychological therapy and aversion therapy, but a pedophile was a pedophile and that was what he wanted to be. That was his sexual preference. Less than three years later Glidewell walked free and immediately reverted to old habits.

By that time George Haralson was a sergeant in SID, head of the unit. One of his undercovers, Detective Steve Odom, made contact with Glidewell and set up a meet to buy some photos of a third grader.

Glidewell hadn't seemed particularly dangerous when Haralson busted him the first time, but prison changed men. Child molestors rode the bottom rungs of any penitentiary's social ladder. Other convicts treated them with contempt, often turned them out as "sissies" for sex. Glidewell passed around that he would die first rather than return to the joint. He told Odom that.

"Yeah, man," Odom agreed in his guise as kiddie pornographer. "That's some real bad shit, man."

Cops took those kinds of threats seriously. Haralson organized the buy carefully. It wasn't going to be easy. Glidewell insisted on having the meet in the big Wal-Mart parking lot on East Admiral Place next to Mingo Creek. It was a Tuesday, a warm, dry afternoon in August when people were getting off work. Wal-Mart and its lot would be crowded.

Haralson stationed a marked black-and-white behind some buildings south of the traffic circle. Three SID undercovers parked in a surveillance van in front of Wal-Mart with the other cars. Haralson and Detective Chris Carmon hid their unmarked on the west side of Wal-Mart. The plan was simple; the best plans always were.

Odom would make the meet unarmed, since he figured Glidewell might pat him down before starting to deal. He was wired, though. As soon as surveillance officers heard the code word "dynamite" over the wire, they would converge on the suspect and conduct a "jump out." They would simply jump out of their cars and grab the guy.

It had always worked before.

Police watched from their various sites about the Wal-Mart parking lot as Glidewell's brown Lincoln Continental separated from the heavy traffic on Admiral and nosed around the parking lot for a few minutes before finding a relatively remote corner near the brushy banks of Mingo Creek. The little creek meandered gently through the middle of the city's east side before it finally dumped into the Arkansas River near downtown. Haralson had no way of knowing how significant to his life the creek was about to become.

A few minutes later, Odom drove into the parking lot in a black GMC pickup. His deep voice sighed over the body mike he wore: "Okay, guys, I'm going on over. Geronimo."

He cruised the parked traffic as though looking for Glidewell. It wouldn't do to go directly to him. Then he waved. He slipped into a space behind the Lincoln and got out of his pickup and into the Continental with Glidewell. The late sun bore into them from across Mingo Creek.

Glidewell was a big man, surly and sullen, and he was in a hurry. He got right down to business. He handed the undercover a brown manila envelope containing eight-by-ten photos of a little brown-haired girl. She was naked and posed suggestively. She wore a puzzled expression.

Surveillance heard the undercover detective draw a deep breath before he got down to business with the pornographer. That was the only indication of the tension inside the Lincoln. Unknown to any of the waiting policemen, the deal was already going hinky. Odom tried to keep from giving away his nervousness, but his eyes kept darting to where Glidewell sat stiffly behind the wheel with his left hand draped out of sight between his door and the seat.

Odom kept thinking *gun.*

He played it cool though. He had been in these situations before.

Listening to an undercover deal go down was singularly unexciting. It sounded like two "good ol' boys" meeting on the street corner to shoot the breeze. It was only *what* they talked about that made the difference.

"Man, this sure is some sweet honey," Odom said, something like that, getting into the rap.

"Told you this little babe was sexy."

"How old you say she is? I don't like 'em too old, you know."

"What does she look like, huh? I told you she was what? Seven? Don't she look it?"

"Man, I'd like to have a little session with her myself."

"That's some private stock, know what I mean? She's just like I told you, ain't she? She's prime pussy. Do you like the pictures or not?"

"Yeah, man. They're just great. And she's sure a little beauty."

Rapping. Working toward a price and an exchange of money to tighten up the case. A lot of softheaded judges thought the crime was not nearly so serious if the guy *gave* the photos away. Even after the buy, the most a kiddie pornographer ever received was about five years in the joint. Of course, five years wasn't really even *five* years. Take three off the five for good time and the like, slash off another year if the convict went to a shrink. That left nine months to a year behind bars.

Cops couldn't expect any more than that. After all, convicted *murderers* only did about seven or eight years. That was the system. That was just the way it was.

Odom's code word rang across the wire, signaling the deal completed. "Man, she sure is a little *dynamite,*" Odom exclaimed.

Haralson snatched his mike: *"Move in."*

The plainclothesmen waited until the uniform car drove into the lot. A suspect was less likely to go squirrelly if he saw a uniform first. Then Haralson and Carmon in their unmarked and the SID van converged, blocking off the Lincoln's escape routes. Doors popped open.

As soon as things started busting, Odom made a grab for Glidewell. The big man's left hand snaked out of hiding. In it flashed a Buck knife with a long, sharp skinning blade. The blade flicked at the undercover, flashing dangerously close to his throat. Unarmed, Odom figured it was time for a little fresh air. He baled out his side of the Lincoln as though propelled by a coiled spring.

Glidewell bailed out the other door. In an instant, everything changed. Suddenly, the cops found themselves held at bay. Crouched like a knife fighter, his blade catching and cutting the raw rays of summer sun, the pedophile snicked and slashed the air in front of him.

"Get back. Get back. I'll cut your fuckin' throats."

The cops became as excited as hounds treeing a bear. Pistols appeared in every hand.

"Watch your crossfire!" somebody shouted.

"No. Just everybody hold your fire!" Haralson commanded.

As SID sergeant, he was senior man. He strode up to the melee carrying a 12-gauge pump shotgun loaded with Double-00 buck.

"Everyone calm down," he soothed. In addition to his duties as SID sergeant, he was also a trained hostage negotiator. He always felt it was much better to talk a man into surrendering than to shoot him into it. He eased toward the distraught pornographer.

"Tommy? Tommy Glidewell, it's me. Haralson."

Haralson saw that Glidewell recognized him. Haralson had treated the guy decently during the first arrest. Glidewell should remember that.

"George, you stay back too. I swear to God, I'll cut you too. You're not sending me back to prison."

The guy appeared freaked; he jumped around on stiff legs like a cornered cur ready to gnaw off its own leg. He slashed the air with his knife and tossed it from hand to hand like some movie knife fighter. The wild man look in his eyes told Haralson he would surely kill someone if pressed.

Private citizens could have just turned and walked off. Dialed 911. Police couldn't walk off. They had to press it. But time was on their side. Time diffused any situation. Reason with a guy like this, Haralson had been taught, get him to talking and sooner or later he laid down his weapon. Haralson had successfully handled things like this before.

He walked slowly toward Glidewell, carrying the shotgun in a nonthreatening manner at his side. You might enter a cage with a tiger, but you never entered it defenseless. Haralson spoke in a calm voice, almost a casual tone, as he advanced.

"Tommy, this is not going to get us anywhere. Just lay down the knife so we can talk about things. I did you right the first time, didn't I? I didn't mistreat you. I'll do you right this time."

Crowds gathered in the parking lot, shading their eyes against the low sun beyond the creek as the drama in the parking lot unfolded. Haralson felt his guts contracting. A guy with a knife like this was bad enough. Let him get into the crowds and lay his hands on a hostage—some kid or a woman—and the police might be out here all night with him. Someone would get hurt then for sure.

Haralson made a useful discovery as he advanced: Glidewell retreated ahead of him, a step or two at a time. The policeman carefully circled to the left and slowly drove the pornographer away from the crowds and toward the creek. The other policemen fell back and made a corridor for them.

Glidewell grew more agitated, not less, as Haralson continued talking.

"Kill me! Kill me, you motherfuckers!" he screeched hysterically. "Go ahead and shoot me! I'm not going back."

He retreated inch by inch, wielding the deadly knife

in front of him. More policemen, including a K-9 officer and his dog, surrounded the knife-wielding man until he was completely encircled. Cops were worse than ordinary citizens. Let something hot go down and they wanted to get in on the action.

"Everybody holster your gun," Haralson ordered curtly. He didn't want cops accidentally shooting each other. He was the sergeant; if it came down to a shot, then he would be the one to take it.

The sergeant poured himself out in words. An intelligent man with a sensitivity that he hid inside like a cancer gradually eating him alive, he prayed silently that this thing would end right.

Why was he thinking about death?

Tommy's not going to give it up. He means it. He'll kill a cop and make us kill him rather than return to prison at Big Mac.

Haralson saw it in the man's eyes. Looking into them was like looking deep into fire and seeing nothing there but more fire.

"Tommy, please? We don't need this. Don't make it worse than it already is."

"Get back! Get back! Kill me!" Glidewell screamed.

The entourage shifted onto the grassy strip of mowed lawn where the pavement ended, then picked up speed on the downhill slope toward the creek. Summer water ran shallow in the stream as it cut around gravel banks and tugged gently at cattails and other water plants. The low sun turned the surface of the water a soft rose color.

"You were my friend the first time, George," Glidewell cried, "but you ain't no more. I'll cut you with this knife the same as I will them other cocksuckers."

He lunged at any policeman who moved too near, striking with the long knife to hack it into flesh. Ten minutes of tension passed. Haralson talked. He tried every approach, from promises to pleading. He wanted this goddamned thing to end. He felt as desperate as a stuck record.

The pornographer retreated into the knee-deep creek, drawing the policemen with him. It was a bizarre scene—a bunch of cops splashing around in a scummy little creek surrounding a crazy man sprung on grasshopper's legs. Cops kept falling in the water, slipping on rocks slimy with moss. The K-9 dog barked and splashed at the end of its leash. Spectators lined the banks of the stream. A KTUL-8 TV cameraman filmed everything for "The Ten O'Clock News."

Haralson noticed little of this; his entire attention focused on Glidewell. Talking wasn't doing much good, he saw. He looked for an opening, some distraction to divert Glidewell long enough for him to lunge underneath the suspect's knife and make a grab. He signaled the K-9 officer to keep his dog barking to occupy Glidewell's attention. He moved to within striking distance of the knife.

Maintaining his distance, less than four feet away from the slashing blade, Haralson maneuvered the cornered pedophile until Glidewell's back was to the far bank of the creek. The policemen formed a rough semicircle to the suspect's front. That provided them a clear field of fire, in case Haralson missed when he charged and someone had to shoot.

Glidewell did a series of kung fu moves, flipping the knife from one hand to another. His gaze fixated on the K-9 officer and his dog. Haralson's leg muscles bunched to spring.

Suddenly, the man's knife arm snaked back like a rattler coiling to strike, the blade poised for throwing. The police had no way of knowing how good he was with the knife. It was Haralson's experience that thugs didn't carry knives in the streets unless they knew how to use them. What the sergeant saw at that instant was that a policeman's life lay in immediate peril.

All systems went on survival instinct. The next three seconds stretched into an eternity of slow motion.

Haralson's shotgun muzzle snapped to waist level. It belched flame and smoke. The charge of Double-OO snatched at Glidewell's off arm while the recoil knocked Haralson's precarious footing out from underneath him.

He jacked in a second round and fired it from midair. Blood exploded from Glidewell's chest.

No man died instantly from gunshot. There was always a second or two that he ran on adrenaline alone, even if his heart was demolished. A man could get to you in that time and kill you before he died.

Haralson hit the water flat on his back. When he came up, sputtering and coughing, Glidewell was almost on top of him, knife upraised, lunging. He had been knocked to his knees in the red-turning water, but the manic mask of his face revealed his dying intent to kill a cop before he succumbed to his wounds.

The fallen cop thrust the length of his shotgun toward the terrible bloody apparition closing on him and fired a third shot at point-blank range. That folded Glidewell. His body slipped beneath the boiling surface of the water. It bobbed facedown on the turmoil. Little worm squiggles of blood stained the water.

George Haralson clambered slowly to his feet. It seemed none of the other policemen had moved. All eyes riveted on the floating body. Haralson stood there for a long minute with the smoking shotgun hanging from the end of his arm and the gentle creek red from the setting sun and Glidewell's blood tugging at the legs of his jeans.

He wanted to run to his house, hide there and get away from it all—the filth, the dirt, the violence. Tears blinded him. He stood there in the creek staring at the body of the man he had just killed. He was crying.

6

The Cops' "Old West" Mentality

In popular versions of the Old West legend, the Western lawman is endowed with a bold jaw, a keen eye, a fast draw, and he always, *always,* lets the badman draw first. Wyatt Earp's gunfight at the OK Corral is better folklore than Lewis and Clark's explorations or Teddy Roosevelt's charge up San Juan Hill. The persona attributed to Wyatt Earp and other famous lawmen like Bat Masterson, Pat Garrett, Ben Williams, and I. L. Gilstrap survives in the modern policeman, whether he's a Boston beat cop or a New Mexico deputy sheriff.

Underneath the average cop's tough shell beats the heart of a genuine romantic. Although he might never admit it, the policeman sees himself as a kind of town tamer who uses his personal skills, judgment, wit, and power to impose law and order on his beat. Station house banter between and among cops is spiced with comments such as: "I walk into this place like Matt Dillon . . ."; "This hemorrhoid thinks he's Billy the Kid, but I Pat Garretted *his* ass . . ."; "For a second there I thought it was the OK Corral all over again."

"Guess I always wanted to be a hero, huh?" a cop said, shrugging off the sentiment. "Standing right out there in the middle of the street like *High Noon* keeping the bad guys from fucking with the good guys. That's me—your average Wyatt Earp. Fucked up, huh?"

Not even the Old West, truth be told, was always a white hat vs. black hat stand-up-and-face-off kind of place. Nothing in real life is ever that simple. Even Wyatt was once charged with murder.

Modern law enforcement is much more complicated than it was in Tombstone, Arizona, or Dodge City, Kansas, where the marshal often decided for himself what was moral and right, law be damned. Today's cop created a paradox for himself in seeing himself as the champion of good standing out in the street fighting it out with evil. He must constantly adjust his Old West image to fit real world realities. A lawman of a century ago, or even fifty years ago, may have gotten by with a questionable shooting because "he meant well and the guy he shot was a scoundrel." Not anymore. If today's town tamer uses deadly force, he had better be right.

"You draw your service weapon," cautioned a Miami police firearms instructor, "you make damned sure it's justified. If you use it, you're talking about an instant in time that's going to change the rest of your life. I know cops right now who are in prison because they screwed up using deadly force.

"You think about that every time you think about drawing your gun. Think about your ol' lady sleeping with some other stiff dick because you drew twenty years in the joint for shooting some scrote that *needed* shooting but you didn't shoot him at the right time for the right reason. You think about it."

A TV cop gets into at least one gunfight on every thirty-minute episode and leaves bad guy corpses stacked up inside the television set. He always assumes the proper firing stance, aims, and blasts away coolly and calmly as though he were about to kiss the heroine. After the gun smoke clears, he is promoted, wins a medal for heroism, and proudly displays the girl on his slightly wounded arm.

It's not often like that in the real cop's world. While violent conflict is always possible, it is not an everyday occurrence. Cops like to say police work is hours and hours of utter boredom followed by sudden stark terror. The policeman must be *willing* to use deadly force, but not *eager* to use it. He never treats violence casually.

This willingness to use force is something the cop straps on before he goes to work, like he straps on his gun and handcuffs. Without it, he might as well turn in his badge. First of all, fellow cops sense a weak cop whom they cannot trust to do the right thing if, say, some gorilla has another cop flat on his butt and is about to cave in his head with a steel fence post.

Bad guys also sense the weak cop, whom they treat with contempt. A weak cop unable or unwilling to stand up like Wyatt Earp and put steel in his enforcement of the law is asking to get hurt.

"The most important thing you got going for you in the streets," continued the Miami firearms instructor, "is a big set of balls. You walk into some blind pit filled with every scummy piece of lowlife this side of *Star Wars* and you *look* like you're the meanest sonofabitch in the valley, you're going to get attention. Nobody's going to fuck with you. You got balls—and, by God, they know it.

"Now, you mince in there like Elmer Fudd, some wise ass is going to try you. He's going to *make* you use force—and if you can't use it the maggots are going to brag around to their shithead buddies how they took on a cop and beat him. That makes it tougher on the next cop who has to take action."

To the Old West sheriff or marshal, the bad guy was a *bad* guy who had to be stopped—*dead or alive*. A sheriff could be forgiven a few excesses if he was protecting citizens against designated outlaws. He didn't have to worry about civil rights lawsuits.

A Philadelphia or New York cop still views outlaws in the same light as Wyatt Earp did. Trouble is, society looks upon the modern criminal as a victim of his environment who must be rehabilitated rather than stopped. A cop who today misjudges and handles a shooting incorrectly may be looking forward to prison stripes or, at least, to an unemployment line.

He still suffers even if he shoots the right guy for the right reason at the right time. The public has a tendency to look with suspicion upon any police shooting, always willing to suppose "cover up" or misconduct. Internal Affairs and a shooting board will investigate the incident as though it were a crime. More than likely the cop will be suspended and the suspension made public, as though he were at least guilty of *something*.

Finally, the cop is probably going to be sued by the dead guy's survivors. Juries have financially ruined good cops, not because the policemen shot improperly but instead because they didn't let the bad guy shoot first or the bad guy was pointing a gun that turned out to be unloaded. Something like that.

Killing a man damages a policeman's humanity. In spite of all the squad room bravado following a fatal police shooting, the officer involved inevitably feels at least some guilt or regret.

"I had to shoot this scrote," a Dallas police officer recalled. "He knifed his wife and his son and he comes at me with the knife. What am I to do? So I let the hammer down on him. All the guys are joking about the poor fucker, taking bets and stuff on when he's gonna die. I went right along with it. I never told anybody how I really felt about it, especially after the dude gave up the ghost.

"I was glad it was him and not me, but I just felt kinda like you'd poured everything out of me. I didn't feel good about it, proud it happened or anything like that. I just felt . . .

"I wanted to go off by myself and sit down and just stare off somewhere. Say what you want, that's how I felt."

None of the Old West lawmen apparently ever felt that way.

7

Officer Bill McCracken, Tulsa, Oklahoma

October 14, 1969, 1:30 A.M.

Most of the time stakeouts were as nonproductive as they were boring. Cops hid waiting for some scum bag who was *supposed* to hit a place, or who *might* hit it. He seldom did. Not while the cops were there to slap him with five-to-twenty at Big Mac, the state pen. So the policemen sat there killing time. Scratching and belching and farting and laughing about it and retelling all the old dirty jokes passed around at squad meetings.

Plainclothesmen Bill McCracken and Jim Lannigan fought off sleep. McCracken eased out of the car and walked in the darkness to the end of the alley. He stamped his feet in the cool night air and flung his arms like a windmill. He had already counted bag ladies and cars with one taillight.

He peered at the Quik Trip located down and across the street at the intersection of Pine Street and Lewis Avenue. Its lights splashed out the wide windows and over the empty parking lot. The clerk inside braced his elbows on the counter and fought his nodding head to keep from dozing off.

"Cocksucker," McCracken muttered to himself.

Not the clerk. The scum bag.

The scum bag—this one a guy wearing a red ski mask—had been knocking off North Tulsa convenience stores like plinking Coke bottles off a fence. More than a dozen of them in the last two months. Always the same MO—*modus operandi,* method of operation. Sweatshirt, black revolver held along his side, red ski mask, and as punctual between ten P.M. and two A.M. as a clock puncher at the Ford Glass Plant.

Why crud picked on convenience stores was something no cop understood. They could make more money digging ditches or something. But that was *work.* McCracken rolled hot on one robbery in which a slime ball shot and killed a clerk for seven dollars. *Seven* dollars for an innocent man's life.

The big policeman with the Marine Corps scar on his lip ambled back to his partner. Lannigan yawned down to about his knees and glanced at his watch.

"Quarter till two," he said. "It's another fuckin' no-show night. Who booked this maggot anyhow? I was all ready for opening night."

He patted his shotgun.

"Wasted night," McCracken agreed. They could have been doing other things. Like raiding the Century Club and busting the nudies and their pimps.

"I could use a little cholesterol," Lannigan continued. "How about the Pancake House? The dude's not hitting tonight. I've seen more action at a Fraternal Order of Police meeting."

Some of the other cops on George Squad—the special plainclothes unit organized to fight major crime down and dirty—were already pulling off their stakeouts and checking out for breakfast. McCracken glanced at the attendant at the Quik Trip down the street.

"Let's go, partner," he agreed. "The only thing that's gonna get that clerk tonight is the sleep monster."

Five minutes later, not even that, the plainclothesmen pulled into the Pancake House parking lot at Third and Utica Avenue. The robbery buzzer going off over their radio gave them a start. They looked at each other.

George Ten and all units in the vicinity—armed robbery just occurred. Quik Trip. Pine and Lewis . . .

"Jesus!" McCracken roared.

Lannigan pounded his fist against the car dash.

Suspect described as a black male, red ski mask . . .

Cops by necessity depended a lot upon the law of averages. The law of averages, for example, said a policeman could do his twenty years on the streets and not get shot or have to shoot somebody. The law of averages also said a cop had about one chance in a hundred of coming up with something on a random stakeout. The averages were better if he had a snitch —or *user friendly* as they were sometimes called in the computer age—but still the averages weighed lopsided against him.

Compute the averages then of staking out for a bandit, missing him the first time like McCracken and Lannigan had done, and then staking out for him again and coming up with anything other than yawns and a sore ass. What were the odds? Maybe a thousand to one? Ten thousand to one?

Three nights after the Pine and Lewis robbery, the downtown complaint desk received a telephone call from the clerk of the Quik Trip on Cincinnati Avenue and Forty-sixth Street North. The bandit in the red ski mask had robbed the store four times in two months, enough for the clerk to discern a pattern.

The same young black man had entered the store early on each of the four nights it was robbed. That was the only time he ever came in. He had been in tonight.

George Squad Sergeant Wayburn Cotton thought the clerk might just be jumpy. The Quik Trip general manager found it increasingly difficult to find employees to work northside stores. Nearly all of them had been held up at least once. The clerks were so wired that if a black kid on a bicycle so much as pedaled across the parking lot after ten P.M. they were on the phone to the police.

"It might just be coincidence that the guy comes in before every robbery," Sergeant Cotton explained to McCracken. "The clerk can't say it's our guy because when he comes back he's wearing the mask. It might not be anything, but the clerk thinks tonight's the night."

McCracken's partner Lannigan had taken the night off.

"I'll get you another partner for the stakeout," Cotton offered.

"Nah. The clerk's just scared. No use two of us getting bedsores on our rumps. Lannigan'll be back tomorrow night."

Shortly before ten P.M. McCracken backed his old undercover Ford into the shadows of a closed service station diagonally across the intersection from the North Cincinnati Quik Trip. He wore his uniform for easy recognition. Just in case. He looked things over before settling in. Another long night and a sore ass.

Two huge steel pillars on the parking lot in front of the store supported the Quik Trip sign. McCracken watched through the large display windows everything that transpired inside the store. Even the clerk didn't realize he was under surveillance until McCracken got the munchies around midnight and slipped across the street to pick up some snacks.

"I feel so much better knowing you're there," the clerk said.

McCracken shrugged. Nothing was going to happen. Three years on the police department, the last of these with the George Squad crime fighters, and the nearest he ever came to catching anyone on a stakeout was when a pizza delivery got the wrong address.

"But if the bandit does happen to come in," he instructed the attendant, "do exactly what he tells you. When you see me coming, just stay out of the way."

Working a stakeout alone was a little like waiting for a bank to open on Sunday. McCracken shifted positions in his car. Yawned. He watched idly as the store attendant walked outside with a broom to sweep the sidewalk.

Suddenly, McCracken's attention focused. A tall black man wearing a ski mask and a gray sweatshirt materialized out of the darkness at the corner of the store. He grabbed the clerk's arm and shoved a blue steel revolver into his ribs before escorting him inside to the cash register.

It was a bit like bear hunting from a stand. You never really believed one would ever show up. But then, suddenly, there he was.

McCracken grabbed his radio mike, knocking potato chips flying all over the car. Long-winded Zebra-81 hung on the air calling in a 10-28 on a possible stolen vehicle.

For Christ's sake, get off the radio. I need a backup. I got a robbery going down—

Zebra-81 droned on. A robbery took about two minutes tops. McCracken dropped the mike and snatched his 12-gauge from its rack. He wanted heavy artillery to go up against another gun. It wasn't fair, but life wasn't fair. He knew this cop one time who emptied his revolver shooting at a sleaze ball less than ten feet away. Missed every shot.

The sleaze ball shot the cop.

Each round of Double-OO buck held the equivalent of nine .32-caliber slugs capable of stopping the meanest grizzly or the most hyped-up junkie. A shotgun was a psychological thing too. Nothing let a punk know you meant business more than racking a round into the chamber of a 12-gauge. *Craaa-nk!* McCracken saw a burglar in a warehouse actually shit in his pants when he heard the sound.

The policeman sprinted across the street and stationed himself behind one of the steel pillars supporting the Quik Trip sign. Inside the store, past the magazine rack and newspaper stand and bubble gum machine, the masked man helped himself to the goodies in the cash register while the clerk cowered in terror.

Then he shoved his pistol into the attendant's face and motioned him toward the back room. He waited by the counter until the clerk disappeared before he shoved the ski mask into a cap on top of his head. McCracken saw a young, clean-cut face. The bandit strode toward the door. He seemed as skittish as a preacher in a whorehouse. Some sound from the back room caused him to swap ends like a cat; his gun snapped up for quick action.

This was a dangerous man. McCracken hoped the clerk stayed put, didn't try something foolish. He didn't want to have to shoot the guy through the plate glass window.

Afterward, it surprised him how calm he remained as he sighted the shotgun on his human target. He still thought the robber would surrender peacefully when he heard *craaa-nk!* Maybe even shit in his pants.

The bandit rushed out the door holding the pistol next to his thigh, still stuffing money into his pockets with the other hand. He had tunnel vision. *Escape* was all he saw. He probably wouldn't have noticed a chartreuse elephant tied up to a battleship.

McCracken stepped into the open so the guy could see his uniform. The bandit hurried south toward the closed service station next door.

"Halt! Police!"

Craaa-nk!

The robber kept walking, but as he did he lifted his gun hand and fired a shot at the officer. McCracken always felt there should be drumrolls or *something* dramatic before a gunfight, just like in the movies. He was almost disappointed in the little spiteful *pop!* and spit of fire, like a snake's tongue, that flicked from his opponent's pistol. The bullet snapped at the air as it went by his head, like it was stealing his breath.

The resounding *boom!* of McCracken's shotgun blended with the bandit's *pop!*

A load of OO-buckshot disintegrates a concrete building block at fifty feet, which was just about the distance between the cop and the robber. McCracken gaped. The robber didn't even flinch. He popped another round at the officer over his shoulder as he accelerated from zero to thirty in about one second.

McCracken couldn't believe he missed. Not at that range with a shotgun. He jacked in a fresh round. The shotgun thundered again.

McCracken was so surprised at apparently missing

again that he stood tall in the open, not even thinking of ducking for cover, and carefully drew a bead on the fleeing criminal. The bandit cut across the service station lot, banging bullets back at the exposed and stationary policeman as he ran.

McCracken held his fire. He took calculated aim while lead whizzed past him.

Carefully this time, he stroked the trigger. The long gun belched flame, momentarily obliterating the officer's view of his target.

The bandit dropped. He went down like Babe Ruth had home-run tested a Louisville Slugger across his ribs.

The guy was *down*. His eyes rolled wild like pinballs. He chewed on his lips.

"I'm hit! I'm hit!" he screamed, panicked. "Get me to a doctor."

McCracken ran over and kicked the wounded man's gun free before he knelt to examine his work. The guy must have been pumping adrenaline through a fire hose. The policeman hadn't missed a single shot. One round of buckshot can stop a five-hundred-pound bear. Of a total of twenty-seven pellets in the three rounds of buckshot fired during the fight, the one-hundred-sixty-pound bandit caught twenty-one of them. They lodged in every vital organ in his body. It was a little like he had been torn apart with a submachine gun. It was always harder to kill a man than most people imagined.

POSTSCRIPT: The bandit, twenty years old, died a half hour after he fell at the service station. A former high school track star, he had never been in any trouble with the police before. On robbery nights, he went to bed with his wife and waited until she fell asleep before he slipped out of bed and drew his street clothing over his pajamas. He made his midnight withdrawals with his .38 and ran back home and crawled into bed again before his wife ever missed him.

McCracken gave him a chance to surrender. "He fucked it up, not me. He intended to kill me; I intended to kill him."

8

Officers Mike Little and Kevin Johnson, Tulsa, Oklahoma

April 5, 1988, 10:00 p.m.

It took a while, as it always did, for the crimes to merge into a recognizable *modus operandi*. An MO is a criminal's signature. If a criminal commits a particular crime for the first time and gets away with it, he has a tendency to commit all future crimes the same way. He may dot an *i* differently or scrawl a different loop onto a *y,* but the basic signature remains his, readily recognized by experienced detectives.

So it was with the brutal burglar and rapist who became known as Tulsa's "Southside Stalker." He and his cronies started out peanuts, but kept building until they terrorized a city.

The crimes began on the night of July 11, 1987, when two gun-toting thugs wearing rubber ape masks robbed a pizza restaurant employee making a cash deposit at a night bank depository. Four days later, July 15, the "Apes" robbed a pizza parlor. On July 21, an "Ape" going it solo heisted a Mexican restaurant on Fifteenth Street. The following night, a seafood restaurant fell in Broken Arrow, a southeast Tulsa suburb.

That was the last of the "Apes." They were replaced by a brace of armed robbers wearing pillowcases over their heads. The "Pillows" robbed restaurants in south Tulsa on each of the nights of July 24, July 26, August 7, and August 8.

Different masks, same MO. As with the "Apes," the "Pillows" surprised restaurant employees late at night, forced them to lie facedown on the floor, and then looted cash registers and safes. They remained firm and methodical, comfortable with the routine they had established. Although witnesses could not see the criminals' faces, they described the intruders as two white males in their twenties. One was relatively short and stocky; the other appeared taller and more slender. The stocky one was in charge.

On the night of August 15, the "Pillows" raised the stakes.

Near midnight, after traffic had thinned out, an attractive young woman attendant of a convenience store on South Sheridan looked up into the gun muzzle of a customer wearing a pillowcase drawn over his head. The assailant swept up the store's receipts before apparently deciding he wanted more than cash. He marched the woman at gunpoint to a vacant apartment in the complex behind the store where he raped her.

The pillowcase gave the suspect away. That and his description as a relatively short and stocky white man.

"It's our guy," said Robbery Detail supervisor Sergeant Don Bell. "I want that asshole stopped."

The night of the rape proved to be the last of the "Pillows," but not of the suspects. Near midnight of August 25, two armed men robbed a sports shop on South Memorial Avenue. They wore masks made of T-shirts with cutout eyeholes.

Two nights later a "T-shirt" abducted a woman off the street and took her to the same vacant apartment on South Sheridan where the "Pillow" had raped the convenience store clerk less than two weeks previously.

Detectives admitted the obvious. The suspects, whoever they were, had progressed from straight armed robbery to robbery with rape to rape alone.

What came next?

Two "T-shirts" stuck up a food store on South Sheridan on September 1. Three days after that, the Southside raping bandits apparently raised the stakes again.

On Sunday, September 4, two kids playing in a wooded vacant lot near Fifty-first Street South stumbled upon the bloodied remains of a young woman soon identified as Christie Leigh Ward. Still in her nightclothes, she had been raped and then shot once in the head with a large-caliber firearm. Her red 1987 Firebird was missing. Police recovered it the next morning. It had been set afire and was still smoldering in an apartment house parking lot on South Mingo Road.

Christie Leigh Ward had been a bartender at a pub near South Yale. She left the club at two A.M. to go home. Shortly thereafter she telephoned the club manager to report her safe arrival. The door to her residence was still ajar after police recovered her body. Nothing inside appeared disturbed.

Was it a random abduction and rape—or was it the "T-shirts"? The press clamored to know. Newsmen had picked up the scent.

"There are certain similarities in the MO," Homicide Sergeant Wayne Allen told the press. "The location where she was abducted is fairly close to where the other attacks took place. Otherwise, we don't know."

Police had a hunch, though. The fact that the perpetrators temporarily abandoned their reign of violence after Christie Ward's slaying added to that hunch. It was as though he—or they—had jumped back to take a breath after this latest escalation from rape to murder. At any rate, the chill autumn winds of approaching winter cooled down the south Tulsa crime spree for over two months.

On November 22, the long-dormant felons struck again. A lone man described as stocky abducted and raped a Broken Arrow woman. He wore a ski mask.

Three weeks passed.

On December 17, the attacks resumed in earnest with another "Ski Mask" rape of a young woman abducted from South Garnett Road. On December 21, two "Ski Masks" robbed a southside restaurant using an MO startlingly reminiscent of the "Apes," "Pillows," and "T-shirts" back in July and August. On December 22, a lone "Ski Mask" snatched a woman and raped her at the same South Sheridan apartment complex where the "Pillow" and the "T-shirt" had previously raped other women.

That cinched it.

"The bastards are back," said a policeman. "Bigger and nastier than ever."

Frightened citizens clogged police telephone lines, demanding action. Sergeants assigned additional detectives to the cases. Uniformed policemen in south Tulsa prowled apartment complexes, placed stakeouts on restaurants, and pulled over scores of vehicles to check suspicious occupants.

The "Ski Masks," undaunted, continued to strike.

On New Year's Eve, a gunman hooded in a ski mask kidnapped a thirty-five-year-old woman from a doughnut shop parking lot. He and a second "Ski Mask" drove her to the apartment complex on South Sheridan where both raped her.

The new year in Tulsa took up where the old one ended—in the middle of a crime wave. January proved a busy month for the thugs. The stockier robber, the leader, struck nine times during the month, either alone or with an accomplice. By this time the media had dubbed him "The Southside Stalker."

On January 4, two "Ski Masks" bulled their way into a residence on Fifty-first Street near South Memorial Avenue. They bound four men with duct tape, raped a woman, and ransacked the house before making their escape.

An attack on January 6 provided police their first substantial clue to identifying the suspects when three armed "Ski Masks" let their names slip while accosting forty-year-old Nancy Colhane and her boyfriend John Tall as the couple necked in Colhane's car behind a bar on South Garnett Road. The assailants bound Tall and locked him in the trunk of Colhane's car, then commandeered Tall's pickup truck. They took the woman to an automatic teller terminal and forced her to withdraw four hundred dollars in cash.

"Do you want to do this like we've done it before?" one of the "Ski Masks" asked the other. "Do you want to take her to the RV park or the apartment?"

They took Nancy to the vacant apartment in the South Sheridan complex where they stole her wedding rings and repeatedly raped her.

"One of them," Nancy remembered, "called the other 'son' and 'Eric.'"

She thought about it for a moment.

"It could have been 'Derek,'" she decided.

Detectives ran a computer printout of the names of all known offenders in the area with first names similar to "Eric" or "Derek." Armed with the list, they began tracking down possible suspects and checking on alibis.

It was slow going. Tedious. The criminals moved much faster. They grew bolder, more reckless.

With two rapes already behind him for the month, the "Stalker" tried again on January 13. His victim tore free and jumped out of his car when he slowed for a traffic signal.

The Stalker failed again, twice, late on the night of January 18. Two women, snatched one after the other off the nighttime streets, each escaped his clutches. Out of apparent frustration, the Stalker mugged a pedestrian of his wallet two blocks away.

"It's like he thinks the city belongs to him and he can go out and take whatever he wants anytime he wants it," complained an exasperated detective.

The Stalker proved more successful on January 19 when he kidnapped a Broken Arrow woman as she got into her car outside a friend's house. He ordered her to drive to an apartment house parking lot south of Broken Arrow where he raped her.

Stalker stories made headlines. News of his crimes —and especially of the murder attributed to him— emptied many south Tulsa streets after nightfall. Citizens dreaded the nights because the nights belonged to *him*.

The Stalker still managed to find pickings.

On January 29 at nine A.M., *three* "Ski Masks" walked up to a seventeen-year-old high school student washing his pickup truck at a car wash near Seventy-first Street and South Memorial. They left him bound with duct tape on a nearby wooded lot.

"We're taking your truck to rob a restaurant," they advised him.

The restaurant was just down the block. The "Ski Masks" robbed it at nine-twenty. The MO matched the MO of the previous "Apes," "Pillows," and "T-shirts."

"That's it," exclaimed Patrol Officer Mike Little, in

whose patrol district many of the crimes occurred. "We've got to do something."

Little requested the formation of a task force. Its mission: Stalk the Stalker. Police Chief Drew Diamond saturated south Tulsa with detectives, officers, and plainclothesmen. More than fifty extra policemen prowled the Stalker's crime territory. Female police decoys invited assault by parking alone, but under surveillance, in darkened apartment complexes.

The Stalker proved cunning. On the last day of January, two men—surprisingly unmasked—raped a woman in Sand Springs, a southwest Tulsa suburb. The victim described one suspect as a stocky, dark-haired man in his twenties. The other was about the same age, only slender and blond.

"I can identify them," the woman promised.

The descriptions and the MO convinced police that the Stalker and his accomplice must have branched out to avoid pressure in their home territory. But, less than a week later, the Stalker returned.

At 3:30 A.M. on February 5, a cold Sunday, seventeen-year-old Margie Dancer and her boyfriend made the mistake of sitting in her car in the parking lot of an apartment complex on South Delaware Avenue, the heart of Stalker territory. A man wearing a tan jacket and a ski mask suddenly materialized out of the night, thrust a pistol against Margie's boyfriend's temple and threatened to kill him. An accomplice garbed in green coveralls and an orange ski mask forced the boy into the backseat of Margie's gold-colored BMW and taped his eyes, ears, mouth, and hands.

In the boldest move yet attributed to the Stalker, the kidnappers drove the young couple to the home of Margie's parents near South Memorial. There they restrained Margie's parents and little sister with duct tape.

While the masked man in green coveralls held the family members and Margie's boyfriend at gunpoint in one bedroom, the other one dragged Margie into another bedroom where he raped her twice.

"I asked him if he was the Southside Stalker," Margie later recounted. "He just laughed at me."

The green-coveralled "Ski Mask" traded places with his partner and raped and sodomized the weeping teenager. Afterward, the suspects fled in Margie's BMW, taking some family jewelry with them.

Margie acted quickly. She dialed 911. Patrolman Keith Fallis spotted the stolen getaway car a short distance away and pursued it south at high speeds. An orange ski mask flew out the car's window.

Hard-pressed, the fugitives cornered hard near Eightieth Street and South Sandusky. The BMW's doors popped open. The driver bolted south through the yards; the passenger ran north. The car crashed into a mailbox.

Patrolmen converged, along with K-9 dog teams and a police helicopter. Optimism soon turned to disappointment. The search ended twelve hours later. Once again, the Stalker owned the night. He committed his crimes, then melted back into city shadows.

Officer Mike Little, the patrolman who called for the task force, spent every spare moment of each shift attempting to catch the Stalker. Headlights doused, he prowled apartments. He mapped out the Stalker's possible escape routes. He hid, he watched, he waited.

Evidence accumulated. The latest crime yielded a ski mask containing a blond hair to go along with the names "Eric" or "Derek." Descriptions from the Sand Springs rape victim supported a detailed composite sketch drawn from Margie Dancer's memory. The gunman in the green coveralls had temporarily removed his mask while he raped her. Margie described him as a slender blond man with a "peaches and cream" complexion.

On February 26, after a three-week hiatus to recover from their near capture of February 5, two "Ski Masks" robbed a restaurant. Five nights later, on March 5, they braced the manager of another restaurant on South Sheridan and made him open his safe. The manager also hit his robbery alarm button. Police chased a black pickup truck away from the scene of the crime. The truck and its three masked occupants escaped once again.

Frustrated detectives continued tracking the Stalker and his accomplices, intent on ending the violent crime epidemic that paralyzed south Tulsa residents. Crime Stoppers coordinators received as many as forty calls an *hour* from people trying to provide information about the infamous criminal who had eluded police for over six months.

On March 12, Lieutenant Jack Putnam received an anonymous telephone call from a mystery man who stated he knew who had robbed at least one of the restaurants. The suspects, said the caller, were a stocky, dark-haired man named Royce Owings and his slender blond cousins named Derek and Steven Burger. Owings owned a black pickup truck. He lived in Broken Arrow.

Names, descriptions, the truck, Broken Arrow— they all fit. Nonetheless, police moved cautiously. The evidence was still not conclusive. It might not carry a jury "beyond a reasonable doubt."

The Southside Task Force put a tail on Owings, a twenty-five-year-old ex-convict previously convicted of burglary. Neither of the Burger brothers had prior felony offenses.

During the month that unmarked cars tailed Owings, undercovers picking him up as he left home and putting him to bed again at night, no new "Stalker" crimes were reported. Police began thinking either they had the wrong man—or they had the right man and he was hinky to his tails. Police called off the tail temporarily.

In April, Lieutenant Putnam's informant called again. He said Owings and the Burgers had let things cool off for a while, but they were preparing to start again. They were casing a restaurant in the vicinity of Thirty-first Street and South Harvard Avenue, but the snitch didn't know which one.

Catching a man in the act of committing a crime was surefire proof. Task Force officers secreted themselves on stakeout at restaurants on South Harvard and on Thirty-first Street. Officer Mike Little, who had devoted so many hours to stalking the Stalker, chose the Wendy's on Thirty-first Street.

By what might be construed as an odd coincidence, Little was hiding with Officer Kevin Johnson in the large rear parking lot of Wendy's on Saturday night, April 5, when a white pickup truck whipped onto the lot next to the eatery. A stocky man wearing a red ski mask and carrying a shotgun jumped from the passenger's side. The driver sped off to circle the block and pick him up after the robbery.

The masked man hurried into the restaurant. There were no customers inside, just employees. Obviously, the bandit had been watching and waiting for such an opportunity.

Adrenaline pumping, Little and Johnson remained concealed. For the safety of restaurant employees, they had no choice but to wait until the heist was over and the Stalker came out. It was a hard wait. After all these months, the man suspected of having committed at least twenty armed robberies, fourteen rapes, one murder, and an array of lesser offenses was busy committing his last crime. Minutes passed. They seemed like hours. Little had worked and waited a long time for the opportunity to snap the handcuffs on the Southside Stalker.

Movement. The masked man appeared in the glass-enclosed foyer whose door opened rearward toward the parking lot and the waiting policemen. Little sprang into view, Johnson beside him, shotguns up and aimed, safeties OFF. About twenty-five yards of empty parking lot separated the policemen from the emerging bandit.

"Police! Halt!" they shouted in unison.

The Stalker's shotgun whipped into firing position as he twisted his body to retreat into Wendy's.

He couldn't be allowed to go back. There were too many potential hostages inside.

"Halt!"

Four shotgun blasts shattered the night. Little fired once, Johnson three times. The masked man dropped in his tracks. Glass from the shattered door and foyer sprinkled onto his still form.

The lawmen approached cautiously. They stood silently looking down upon the buckshot-riddled corpse of the notorious criminal who had terrorized south Tulsa—Royce Owings, the Southside Stalker, recently deceased.

POSTSCRIPT: Steven Burger, twenty-four, and his brother Derek, twenty-six, were eventually convicted of some seventeen felonies associated with the Stalker crimes and sentenced to life imprisonment.

"He had a beautiful wife," Steven Burger remarked of his cousin Royce Owings. "He had a nice life. Royce got his kicks doing armed robberies. He got his kicks going out and being wild. He didn't go out drinking and he didn't do drugs. I think he might have been better off if he had gotten his kicks on drugs instead of what he was doing."

One of the Stalker's rape victims attended his funeral.

"I just had to be sure that monster was really gone," she said. "I had to see for myself that the Stalker wouldn't be stalking anyone else."

9

Gun Control

It was shift change at the Kansas City police department, but it could have been any other police department in the nation—Los Angeles, Seattle, Detroit. Cops drove their private cars onto the station lot, parked them, and went to retrieve their black-and-whites. A number of family Chevrolets and Fords and Nissans displayed bright bumper stickers next to Fraternal Order of Police emblems: *When Guns Are Outlawed, Only Outlaws Will Have Guns;* and, *I'll Give Up My Gun When They Pry My Cold Dead Finger Off the Trigger.*

"I don't want these cocksuckers taking my gun away from me," grumbled an officer built square like an armored personnel carrier. "I want to protect *myself* because I know the government can't do it. I don't want my wife leaving home without a gun. And I don't want to take any guns away from citizens either. I'm out there every night and I know—I *know*—that if they don't protect themselves, we cops can't."

Policemen, who know most about firearms carnage,

stand almost unheard in the center of the controversy on gun control. While most of them are authoritarian when it comes to criminals, whom they believe should be kicked in the balls and thrown in jail to rot, they are virtually libertarian when it comes to themselves and other "good citizens." The average street cop realizes through experience that police cannot prevent much crime. Citizens must protect themselves. Men who cannot or will not defend their lives, possessions, and liberties from other men or groups of men soon forfeit them. That's a basic historical truth.

Guns for hunting and for protection on the frontier were a necessary part of settling the New World. The colonists' success in the War for Independence rested largely upon the fact that almost every citizen in the new land owned personal weapons and knew how to use them. It would have been unthinkable for the pragmatic, common-sense framers of the Constitution to intend the control or banning of personal weapons. Even suggesting it would have led to a new revolution.

Besides, the writings of Thomas Jefferson and other colonists suggest they believed personal arms were necessary as one of the checks and balances to preserve liberty and prevent excesses by government. After all, European monarchs and despots had strived for centuries to keep weapons from commoners out of fear that, if armed, the citizens would feel bold enough to resist oppression.

The assassinations of John F. Kennedy, Martin Luther King, and Robert Kennedy in the 1960s prompted an outcry for gun control. The outcry has grown with the appearance of crazies like Patrick Purdy who emptied an assault rifle onto a crowded school playground. More than thirty thousand deaths are tallied each year in the United States as a result of firearms. *Time* magazine gave a blow-by-blow account of a "typical" week—May 1–7, 1989—that claimed 464 gun deaths. Sarah Brady became champion of the gun control lobby after her husband, the White House press secretary, was gunned down along with President Ronald Reagan and left partially paralyzed.

"Are we as a nation going to accept America's bloodshed, or are we ready to stand up and do what is right?" Sarah Brady demanded. "We can prevent the 1990s from being bloodier than the past ten years . . . Let us enter a new decade committed to finding solutions to the problem of gun violence. Let your legislators know that voting with the gun lobby—and against public safety—is no longer acceptable. . . ."

To policemen, the argument that *guns* cause violence is like attacking automobiles for causing traffic mayhem. Attempting to take guns away from everyone in order to prevent their misuse is like burning a house to destroy termites.

Policemen tell an old joke about the criminal justice system in which an overprotective mother advises the school headmaster to beat little Johnny whenever her pampered Rodney does anything wrong.

"Why should I do that?" asked the astonished headmaster.

"Because," explained Rodney's mother, "if you beat Johnny, Rodney will see that he did wrong and won't do it again."

Instead of punishing Rodney for his own sins, society continues to punish Johnny as an example. Many states have passed laws against the purchase and ownership of so-called Saturday night specials—cheap handguns. Several cities have passed laws banning *all* handgun ownership. Some politicians are already advocating outlawing *hunting*. If hunting is outlawed, no one can claim the need for *any* guns.

"With all the violence and murder and killings

we've had in the United States," said Robert Kennedy five minutes before his fatal encounter with a scruffy drifter in a Los Angeles hotel kitchen, "I think you will agree that we must keep firearms from people who have no business with them."

Policemen daily fight the war in the streets against well-armed criminals. Many of them lose their lives each year. Yet, they ask skeptically, how do you keep guns out of the hands of a Sirhan Sirhan without taking guns away from everyone?

There are more than fifty million handguns scattered across the United States, and at least three times that many other firearms. There is no way to retrieve them short of using a gigantic magnet. Like the failure of Prohibition, a ban on handguns would be widely disregarded, unenforceable, and successful only in alienating large blocks of Americans and further destroying the nation's moral fiber.

Besides, restricting or banning firearms *might* make it a little more difficult for a mugger to get a gun—*but he would still get it.* Gun control affects only the honest, ordinary citizen who wants to keep a weapon in the house for protection.

"The notion that more gun laws would deter crime is unadulterated bullshit," a cop said. "Look at all the laws we got against thieving and dope. It's obvious that we can't even properly enforce them. What we need to do is concentrate on putting criminals away when we do catch them. Instead, we slap criminals on the hand—'Don't do that no more, hear?'—and then we slam society across the head. That's really fucked up."

Proponents of gun control like to use statistics to prove that guns are more dangerous to the owners' households than to any potential intruders. Cops know better. Statistics show only those intruders who are actually killed in comparison to suicides, accidental gunshots, and family violence. What statistics never show are assailants who are wounded, captured, or frightened off by gun owners defending themselves and their property. Nor do statistics show the number of criminals who are *deterred* because prospective victims might be armed.

A Tulsa police detective nabbed a gang of burglars who had terrorized the city. He asked them why they selected certain houses and homeowners to rob over others. One of them cried, "What do I look like? A fool? When we cased out places we looked for people who had guns and might use them. We stayed away from those places."

An incident that occurred to a woman and her girlfriend who lived in a Chicago housing project reinforces the police's point that people have to be able to protect themselves.

"I always carried my gun in my hand when I came home because it's dangerous in that building," the woman said. "They'll rape you in the elevators. They'll hit you. They'll take your money. Somebody gave me the gun when I moved into the apartment in August. I'm not telling who, but I always had it out."

One evening a man broke into her apartment. He raped the girlfriend and tossed her out the fifteenth-floor window. A canopy broke her fall and saved her life, although she was critically injured.

The woman returned home about that time, unaware of what had just happened.

"I was coming up the elevator, and, of course, I had my gun out."

She found the door to her apartment splintered.

"I ran to my neighbor's apartment and asked her if she had a phone so I could call the police. But she didn't have a phone. So I walked back and this young man poked his head out of my screen door."

The woman fired one shot. The intruder fled. Undoubtedly, the gun saved her from a fate even worse than that which had befallen her roommate.

Criminals may be cavalier with the lives of others, but they have great fear of losing their own. Cops have noticed the interesting phenomena of how the crime rate in a neighborhood plummets whenever a criminal is shot and killed by police or a victim.

"History repeatedly warns us that human character cannot be scrubbed free of its defects through vain attempts to regulate inanimate objects such as guns," said a former NRA executive vice president. "What has worked in the past, and what we see working now, is tough measures that punish the incorrigible minority who place themselves outside the law. Tough laws designed to incarcerate violent offenders offer something gun control cannot—swift, sure justice meted out with no accompanying erosion of individual liberty."

Most cops agree. They realize the hazards of the job, but they also realize that slapping Johnny to punish Rodney is a compromise to freedom in the name of security.

"I'm a cop because I want to prevent victims, not make victims," said Kansas City police Sergeant Jim Wycoff. "I'll take the chance of facing criminals with guns to prevent ordinary citizens from having to face them unarmed if gun control has its way."

One Californian may have struck to the heart of the gun control issue in describing how his house was burglarized, his car vandalized, and his wife threatened before he finally resorted to carrying a gun for protection. He proved the old saw that a conservative is a liberal who has been mugged.

One night, five knife-wielding thugs accosted him and demanded money.

"Just the wallet, man. Won't be no trouble."

This time, there was a difference in the Californian.

His mind filled with thoughts that would never have occurred to him before.

Don't you see how you're misreading me? he thought. *I used to be a victim, but now I'm not. Can't you see the difference?*

The concept he hit upon—that of *not feeling like a victim*—may prove to be the central issue in the heightened debate over gun control.

10

Officer Chuck Sasser, Miami, Florida

August 8, 1968, 4:30 P.M.

Long, hot summers. Cops dreaded them. Kids in the ghettos busted open fire hydrants to get to the water. Tempers crackled in the summer sun. Glaring Black Panthers in their berets and black garb swaggered around Goodbread Alley daring the passing cops to so much as glance at them.

Gangs burned any patrol cruiser left parked too long unattended. Black youths in the projects dropped concrete blocks on top of patrolling green-and-whites. An occasional sniper popped out the tires of police cars. Revolutionaries lured a twenty-one-year-old rookie cop into a trap and shot him through the head long-distance with a rifle. Threatening graffiti smeared the rotted pastel walls in the ghettos: *White Man, Your Time Is Near. Black Power; My Man Is Stronger Than Samson, He Can Whip Five Cops.*

The latest round of rioting started with Watts and spread, showering out like sparks from a green wood campfire to ignite in Newark, Detroit, Atlanta . . . The threat of riot became an obligation to riot. Cops held their breaths and checked their combat gear every time someone organized a protest. The poor cop, confused by it all, uncertain about what was expected of him—he ended up in the middle. Damned if he did, damned if he didn't.

Riot matured in a predictable pattern, quickly progressing from speeches to something ugly piled up like kindling in the slums, requiring only a spark to set it off. Most often, the policeman provided the spark.

Like in Tampa on June 11, 1967, when patrolmen surprised three black men fleeing from a burglarized warehouse. One of the cops shot and killed one of the burglars. Riot followed.

Or like in Cincinnati. Police arrested a black jazz musician named Posteal Laskey for raping and murdering middle-aged white women. Blacks rioted over his conviction in May 1967.

In Newark it was a cab driver who resisted arrest. Twenty-three people died in the violence that followed in July 1967, including a police detective and a fireman.

Forty-three people died in Detroit in rioting that started with a police raid on a Blind Pig, an illegal after-hours club.

In Miami, Florida, police had been predicting riot for the past several summers. "Black leaders" promised it. There would never be a better time for it than when the Republican National Convention opened in Miami Beach in August. Everything was set for it, all the actors in place. Police Chief Walter Headley's "Get tough on criminals" policy was the talk of the nation. Civil rights groups attacked the policy as racist.

"Bullshit," the tough old chief snarled. "Criminals don't have color."

Nervous lieutenants and captains rarely seen away

from their desks slipped down to patrol squad meetings to reassure the troops.

"You know what the Chief's 'Get Tough' policy is. We're not backing down. The law is the law. Enforce it fairly and equally."

"What if we have to shoot?"

"Make sure it's justified, then drop the hammer. They are not going to burn Miami and get away with it like they have everywhere else."

"Oh, they're gonna burn it all right," a patrolman muttered from the ranks. "The bastards are really gonna burn it this time."

Sergeants cautioned their men: "Be careful out there. Don't get into any place you can't get out of. Don't go anywhere alone, not even on a vandalism report. Remember, no matter what happens, *you* are going to get the blame for it."

On the morning the Republican Convention began, August 6, 1968, Patrol Officer Chuck Sasser drew paddy wagon duty with another uniform named Evans. The two cops waited in Bayfront Park, across Biscayne Bay from Miami Beach, and listened to radio reports giving the progress of a protest "mule train" rambling down Collins Avenue. The "mule train" consisted of a team of mules pulling a farm wagon. It was supposed to signify the plight of the poor, most of whom had never even seen a team of mules.

When crowds spooked the mules into stampeding, it sparked a rumor that undercover police were behind it to discredit civil rights protests. Rumors continued flying in the charged atmosphere, fanning sparks into brushfires of rage and violence in Liberty City, the Central District, and in Coconut Grove. To Sasser, most of the afternoon passed like sound bites from a TV news report.

Confrontations between uniformed and helmeted police and mobs of angry blacks led to further confrontations. Sasser stood shoulder to shoulder with other policemen in a long show of force in front of projects on North Sixty-second Street. A gang of young blacks broke out of the project and raced down the street breaking windows and setting off burglar alarms. The police captain on the scene did not want to be accused in the aftermath of overreacting. The cops stood there and watched helplessly while the gangs in the streets multiplied into mobs. Soon, black smoke billowed into the sunset from burning cars; looters surged off into side streets to bust into markets, hardware, and liquor stores. The liquor stores were the hardest hit.

"Are we having fun yet? Is it a riot yet?" Evans quipped.

Police brass responded by setting up a command post in a park on Fifty-second Street. They broke the policemen into four-man teams and assigned them to randomly running the riot zone, scooting from alarm to alarm and chasing looters into the gathering darkness. By full nightfall, patrolmen were carrying cases of tear gas grenades and boxes of .30-caliber carbine and 12-gauge shotgun ammunition to the trunks of their cars.

"They've declared war on the police out there!" announced a sergeant brandishing a pump shotgun.

Miami had never had a riot. Police were ill-prepared for it, both logistically and tactically. For example, the department was well stocked in tear gas, but had no gas masks. Cops confronted mobs of looters by hurling gas grenades at them and then speeding away.

Near midnight, while Liberty City teemed with unruly humanity, more than one hundred policemen started at one end of Sixty-second Street in a wedge bristling with hardwood 36-inch riot batons and swept the entire length of the street. The sweep quickly deteriorated into disorganized chaos as cops battled several thousand rioters, hardwood batons against broken street signs, tree limbs, baseball bats. Sasser fell to his knees, momentarily stunned by a club bouncing off his helmet. He sprang up in time to catch a fat man in the groin with the end of his stick. He kicked the man in the teeth, then parried a jack handle whistling toward his own face.

Thrusting and jabbing furiously. Shrieking, cursing bodies. Screaming.

Dante's Inferno, Sasser thought.

Afterward, the streets settled into the quiet darkness because all the lights had been broken. But the riot was not yet over. Mattresses and furniture mushroomed overnight into snipers' barricades on the outside walkways of the high-rise tenements. When the looting started with the sunrise, snipers armed with .22s and other Saturday night specials opened up on police.

Some of the snipings became what Norman Mailer called "like firefights in Vietnam." Police return fire crackled fiercely on a side street off Sixty-second. Sasser crouched behind the trunk of his patrol car and peered up through bright morning sunlight at the project buildings looming high above. Windows on the fifth and sixth floors exploded as cops poured a heavy fusillade of fire into them. Voices inside screamed and shouted.

Sasser gripped the .38 revolver he had fired only once in combat during his four years with the department. He had shot off a killer's top lip. But that was different. That was an incident involving a fleeing felon.

This was a firefight. A battle.

Sasser held his fire, seeking a target.

A young black darted out of an alley opening into the street. Sunlight glinted off a bottle. The flaming wick of a Molotov cocktail whooshed as the home-made bomb sailed through the air toward the nearest patrol car. Tentacles of flame shot out from the explosion. Sasser felt the sudden heat against his face and bare arms, momentarily experiencing relief at not having gone up like a human torch.

He flung himself forward across the trunk of his car to brace his gun hand as the bomber turned to run. His shot gouged brick dust out of the wall inches behind the running man. At the same moment, a bullet fired from the projects slicked a shiny spot in the car trunk next to the officer's head. The ricochet shrieked straight into the high sun.

Two close calls in the matter of three or four seconds. Sasser dropped to cover behind the car, braced his back against the tire. Sweating, gripping his .38, squinting through the sweat for the sonofabitch who had tried to kill him while he was trying to kill someone else.

Fucked up. This whole thing is fucked up. . . .

The crescendo of gunfire increased, then tapered off to silence. Bullet holes pockmarked the project high-rises. Glassless windows gaped. From out of nowhere appeared a fat black man on crutches. Bare feet left bloody footprints on the street from his having walked on broken glass. He hobbled directly down the street among the police cars and the stunned cops.

"You is shit-eatin' muthafuckas!" he roared. "Honkies! Cocksuckers! Dog puke! Muthafuckas!"

The guy had a repertoire.

"Shoot me, muthafuckas!" he challenged. *"Shoot me! Shoot me!"*

Cops fidgeted. But no one shot him.

Remarkably, no one else had been shot either. That wasn't to last. A policeman in the Central District received a flesh wound through the shoulder. A young cop named Cosgrove, one of the four-man team that included Sasser, shot a teenager running from a looted building, blasted him with 00-buckshot through the legs. The cops dragged him to their patrol car and propped him in the backseat between Evans and Sasser. Ambulances refused to enter the riot zone. The wounded kid left a pool of thick blood on the floorboard.

Police firing .30-caliber carbines honed in on a sniper perched on a billboard on top of a building. The sniper leaped off, shattering both legs. Cops killed a black looter on Second Avenue. On Twelfth Avenue, mobs trapped four policemen in an alley and bombarded them with concrete blocks, bricks, lids cut from coffee cans, rubber balls studded with razor blades. Bleeding and desperate, the policemen spread-eagled a prisoner to the top of their patrol car and held him there as a shield while they drove to safety.

By midafternoon, fire gutted buildings dotted Sixty-second Street. Broken glass sparked in the sun. Burglar alarms warbled. Laughing men, women, and even very young children pushed shopping carts filled with looted TVs and appliances, canned goods, and toys.

Sasser shouted at two little boys, each no older than five, who struggled to drag a console TV out the back door of an appliance store.

"You kids drop that and get your little butts home."

One of the kids flipped off the cop. "Fuck you, pig," he shouted.

He probably wasn't even in kindergarten yet.

The government low-rental housing project that consumed much of the north side of Sixty-second

Street was a staging area for looters. The project consisted of a maze of single-story tri- and quadplexes partitioned off with high concrete walls. It stretched several blocks wide and several more deep. Hundreds of people massed among the walls and buildings. Looters scurried from the project, did their thing, then rushed back to their holes like rats. It would have taken a fully armed combat platoon to clear the project. Sniper fire drove back any cops who attempted to enter it.

Late in the afternoon a standoff occurred when mobs from the project attacked policemen flushing looters across the street. Three police cars lined up along the street in front of the housing. Cops ducked a barrage of fire bombs and rocks while an officer with a bullhorn bellowed for the crowd to back off and disperse. Tension crackled in the air like static lightning. Officer Sasser felt it as he knelt behind a car, weapon drawn.

Suddenly, a single gunshot barked from the buildings behind the swirling mobs. The cop with the bullhorn screamed. Sasser, thinking the cop had been hit, darted forward and knelt behind a palm tree. Other policemen hurried into a long skirmish line, seeking cover behind palms, abandoned junker cars, garbage cans.

Gunshots on TV and in the movies are weak sounding, muted, swishing. In real life they are like claps of raw energy released from the depths of the cosmos. It's like each one is punching a hole through the universe. Officer Sasser felt breathless, drained, as the hot summer air filled with the ragged bursting of gunfire. Homicide investigators later identified eleven bullet holes through window and door screens where gunmen had opened fire on police.

The mob dispersed like old smoke in a wind, people

running and screaming to hide behind concrete walls and stucco buildings. Policemen anonymous in helmets and face shields poured bullets into the project. It would have been a massacre if they had been shooting to kill. Instead, frightened and angry, they riddled the walls to relieve tension as much as to drive back the mobs.

Although everything happened in seconds, the seconds passed as slowly as slices of life.

Sasser spotted a black man in khakis jump up from behind a hedge. His little pistol popped, sparking at the muzzle. It was suicide. A cop's bullet smashed into his bulls-eye center. He did a comic flip and sprawled into the hedges. He didn't move again, ever.

The firing continued, but Sasser held his, waiting. He felt both shock and amazement that something like this—a Vietnam firefight—could be fought in the streets of an American city. If it had come to this, a real shooting war, then surely the long-talked-about revolution had begun.

Another black man jumped up from somewhere, apparently driven from cover by the intensity of police fire. He wore green work clothing and had a pistol in his hand as he raced across the open space between walls. Sasser didn't think; he reacted. He quickly centered the sights of his .38 on the gunman's chest and squeezed off his second round of the riot.

The impact of the bullet jolted the running man. It was like he faltered an instant, stumbling, before he caught himself. He disappeared behind the nearest wall.

The shooting ended as suddenly as it began. A barrage of tear gas grenades followed. People driven from hiding emerged from the noxious cloud like tear streaked zombies, coughing and sputtering. Among them stumbled the wounded man in green work clothing. Sasser slowly stood and watched as the man staggered forward, tatters of gas clinging to his clothing, his chest splotched in wet raw blood.

God, Sasser thought, *I did this to him. Damn him. Damn him.*

Don't die, Sasser thought. *I don't want to have killed you.*

It seemed to take willpower and extraordinary effort for the man to place one foot in front of the other. He stared straight ahead. His lips moved, but no words came out. He lurched unsteadily as he passed slowly through police lines, as though toward a destination no one else saw. Silence as profound in its own way as the clatter of gunfire that preceded it hung thick and stale in the air.

Sasser's revolver suddenly assumed the weight of a 105-howitzer. It took all his strength to holster it. He couldn't take his eyes off what he had done.

The wounded man sank slowly to his knees. Then he pitched forward onto the street. He was dead by the time Sasser and another policeman reached him. They dragged the body to the nearest patrol car and shoved it into the backseat. The patrol car wouldn't start. Another car gunned up behind it and locked bumpers. It pushed the patrol car speeding down Sixty-second.

The last policemen saw of the dead man was his bare foot sticking out an open back window. He had lost his shoe in the street when he was being dragged. Since then, every time Sasser thinks of the man he killed he sees the bare foot sticking out the window with the sunlight on it.

No face. Just that foot.

POSTSCRIPT: Officer Chuck Sasser's wife—soon to be ex-wife—looked at him strangely after that.

"How can you kill someone and it not bother you?" she cried, appalled. "What has happened to you?"

Sasser looked at her and walked off. She wouldn't have understood had he tried to explain. He wouldn't have understood it either a few years before when he walked past Big John the armorer and received his issued .38 Smith & Wesson that soon became as much a part of him as his skin.

"I am going to make a man out of you," Training Officer McFann had promised. "A police*man*. A police*man* is tough. A police*man* is at war. In the streets you are *The Man*."

The Man did what he had to do.

11

Officer Dennis Johnson, Tulsa, Oklahoma

March 2, 1976, 8:00 A.M./March 27, 1977, 1:00 A.M.

Any policeman who retires with the comment that he never even had to *draw* his gun during twenty years on the job probably rode a desk or worked a school crossing for most of his career. During one single year alone, Tulsa Patrol Officer Dennis Johnson went for his gun *twice*.

Johnson, a SWAT team member and a former K-9 officer, had an uncanny ability for nabbing felons. In the streets working a district uniform car, he kept constantly on the prowl, recovering more stolen cars and collaring more burglars than any other patrolman on his shift. Over the years he developed a network of snitches who kept him well informed of underworld activities.

One morning in early March an informant passed him word that a prison escapee named Timothy Prock was hiding out on the east side at his girlfriend's house. Policemen looked upon Prock as the most dangerous punk in Oklahoma. At age twenty-six, he had already been convicted of sixteen separate felonies. The last time he escaped from prison, three years ago, he tried to shoot Officer Jack Sherl when police cornered him. Sherl got off his shot first and wounded Prock.

This time, Prock was boasting he would not be taken alive again.

Johnson, his district backup Larry Clayton, and two other patrolmen quietly surrounded a small frame house on Thirteenth Place in east Tulsa. Early mornings were the best time to go after fugitives. They never held steady jobs. They stayed up nights smoking dope or drinking and trying to make some score or another, then slept during the day.

A skinny brunette with drab, stringy hair met Johnson and Clayton at her door. She glared at the policemen through red-rimmed eyes and kept sniffling. Probably a junkie. Probably a barroom whore.

"Timothy ain't here," she said.

"Yeah. Sure," Johnson replied. "But you can be held responsible if he is here and you're hiding him and somebody gets hurt."

"He ain't here," she insisted, rubbing her eyes and sniffling and looking sullen. "What time is it anyhow? I ain't even had coffee. It's cold out here."

Johnson's dark eyes bore hard into the woman's. A tall, dark-haired man with a flaring mustache, he could be intimidating.

"I think you're lying," he said bluntly. "Mind if we come in and look for ourselves?"

The woman hesitated.

"We can always leave someone here to watch the place while we go get a search warrant," Johnson pointed out. "Then we'll arrest you too for harboring a fugitive."

The brunette stepped aside without protest. She looked bored as the policemen palmed their revolvers and entered the house along a short, dark hallway reeking of garbage held too long indoors. They silently approached two doors facing each other in the hall-way. The door on the left was closed. Clayton opened it, standing to one side, then slipped into the bedroom beyond. Johnson took the other doorway, advancing through a bathroom that opened on the other side into a second bedroom.

Street cops learn to develop instincts that help them stay alive. Johnson, if asked, could never have explained why he knew someone lurked in the darkened bedroom. He just *felt* it. Every sense came alive and vibrating. He eased around the doorjamb until, with one eye, he spotted a mound of covers on the bed. Because of the drawn window shades, he couldn't make out if the mound was a sleeping man or simply pillows.

The mound itself resolved his uncertainty. It came alive. A man erupted in the middle of it, a .38 revolver in his hand. The gun boomed once in the contained space. The muzzle flash blinked-unblinked the room into relief, like a subliminal suggestion.

The *thwack!* of the bullet striking the doorjamb next to Johnson's face drove the cop back. The report from the gun deafened him. Wood splinters stung his face.

Clayton rushed to his partner's rescue.

"Stay back, Larry. I'm okay," Johnson shouted, his back pressed to the wall in the bathroom. "It's Prock with a gun. He's in the bedroom."

Criminals, as any cop knew, were basically craven backshooters. They talked big and swaggered a lot in barrooms, but when it came down to it they were nothing but cowards.

Prock threw his gun out of bed like a lousy lover and screamed desperately that he wanted to surrender. It was one thing shooting at a cop by surprise, quite another shooting at one prepared to shoot back.

Afterward, with Prock facedown and handcuffed on the floor, Johnson took a long serious look at the bullet hole in the doorjamb. Another two inches to the right and the slug would have smashed through his face.

"That's closer than I ever want to come again," he commented with a long sigh.

Officer Johnson apprehended a number of other desperate criminals that year. The Oil Capital Chamber of Commerce named him its Policeman of the Year, one of the most prestigious awards a Tulsa street cop could receive. In March almost exactly a year following the Prock shooting, Johnson came up hard against a criminal who proved almost as desperate and dangerous as Timothy Prock.

Local narcs and federal drug agents had cracked down on narcotics suppliers in northeastern Oklahoma, a campaign that seriously stemmed the unchecked flow of dangerous drugs. Junkies unable to "get well" on the streets sought alternatives. Tulsa pharmacies became targets of junkies crazed for *anything* to appease the monkeys on their backs. Robbers brutally pistol-whipped several victims and took a shot at a pharmacist who tried to run.

Detectives issued requests for beat patrolmen to keep a close eye on drugstores on their beats, especially the all-nighters. Johnson checked the two pharmacies in his district several times a night, sometimes sitting in his car in an alley or darkened parking lot to watch. The night his vigilance paid off was the most unlikely of nights.

February had thawed into the March drizzlies. Rain fell, cold and steady, turning the graveyard shift even darker than usual.

"Won't be any thieves out tonight," policemen joked as they reported on-duty. "Thieves don't like to be uncomfortable when they work. It's against their union rules."

Johnson took no chances. He forked his black-and-white and made a quick tour of his near-southside beat, checking businesses, before he settled down to prowling for suspicious persons. Thieves were like cockroaches that slithered out of the woodwork when the lights went off.

It was going to be a slow night. Only one man walked the deserted main drag that was Utica Avenue, and he sought cover in St. John's Hospital—an employee reporting for the late shift. It was like The Bomb had dropped on the city, destroying all life while leaving structures intact.

At one A.M., an hour after going on duty, the bored policeman doused his headlights and crept his cruiser through the sprawling shopping mall at Utica Square. Movement seen through the glass front of the twenty-four-hour pharmacy on the other side of Twenty-first Street caught his attention. Falling rain hissing on the pavement drowned the noise of his car engine. He shot across the street to investigate, easing the black-and-white along behind a thick hedge that bordered the pharmacy's parking lot. He braked and stepped out into the rain for a better look.

Although moisture fogged the drugstore's plate glass, the officer's gaze penetrated to where three customers and the store's two night-shift employees, one of them female, were being held at gunpoint against a wall inside. The gunman wore ominous dark glasses and a gray sweatshirt with the hood pulled like a tunnel around his face. He kept an eye and his pistol on his victims while he rifled drugs off the shelves behind the counter.

"Armed robbery in progress, Twenty-first and Utica," Johnson radioed, then retrieved his 12-gauge shotgun from its dash mount. He racked a round of 00-

buckshot into the chamber. He crouched in the wet shadows of the hedge and waited for the bandit to come out. A less-experienced officer might have jeopardized innocent lives by charging into the store, gun blazing.

Johnson had counted on the robber running out of the store alone to a waiting getaway car. Instead, it turned out the junkie didn't even have a vehicle. He planned to steal a customer's car parked on the lot.

"Shit!" Johnson muttered as the bandit exited clutching the arm of the female employee. He carried the revolver in his other hand and his loot inside his sweatshirt.

Criminals were notoriously myopic when it came to escaping from a crime scene. They saw only one thing—their escape route. Johnson pressed himself into the shadows, his thoughts racing. He couldn't let the bandit escape; he couldn't jeopardize the woman's life either. He watched, hoping for an opportunity.

The gunman shoved his captive into the passenger's side of the customer's car, then trotted around to the driver's side. Johnson picked his chance. He sprang into the open so the woman could see his green uniform.

"Get outa the car!" he shouted at her.

Fortunately, the woman was just as quick to act as to think. The car door flew open. She bailed out headfirst onto the rain slick concrete, where she huddled close to the ground out of the line of fire.

The bandit whirled like a dancer and snapped his loaded .38 into firing position. Johnson was already sighting down his shotgun barrel.

A streak of flame riding on a thundering explosion stabbed the rain. The gunman dropped facedown into a puddle of water.

It ended that quickly, in an instant, but Johnson remembered it afterward in slow motion. He simply reacted to training. Normal time returned after the wounded man started moaning and whimpering: "Help me. Help me, please. I've been shot."

POSTSCRIPT: The bandit was twenty-three years old and had just been paroled from the state penitentiary where he was doing time for assault with a deadly weapon. He survived the policeman's shotgun blast to return to prison.

As for Timothy Prock, who twice attempted to murder policemen, a district judge sentenced him to serve an additional forty years in jail. Forty years normally means three or four years actually behind bars. However, the State Pardon and Parole Board receives a letter from Tulsa Policeman Dennis Johnson every time Prock's name appears on the parole docket. The letter points out Prock's numerous previous criminal convictions and protests his release.

"He'll get out some day," Johnson noted. "The next policeman who runs up against him might not be as lucky as Jack Sherl and I were."

12

Officer Dallas Williams, Washington, Pennsylvania

May 5, 1985, 12:15 A.M.

Occasionally, some actor stuck up a convenience store or rolled a drunk on North Main. There were the usual family squabbles on the weekends, and an isolated residential or business burglary. Otherwise, the midnight shift in Washington, Pennsylvania, was about as dead as the old steel mills in nearby Pittsburg. The shift lieutenant often climbed into a squad car with one of his four on-duty patrolmen in order to have company. The graveyard shift in Washington was aptly named.

Lieutenant Ed Cochran yawned and stretched in the passenger's seat of the patrol car driven by Dallas Williams, a muscular black officer who had routine-patrolled the little city for the past five years. The two men had been talking sports and women and cop business. The usual. Keeping each other reasonably alert as they crept into alleys looking for break-ins, nosed around the few all-night businesses, and checked out the light traffic on Main.

Washington wasn't Pittsburgh; the shit came down in Pittsburgh; cops were killed in Pittsburgh.

"How about a cup of coffee or something?" the lieutenant suggested.

Cops and coffee. Like Dick and Jane, salt and pepper, ice cream and cone.

"Sounds good."

Williams checked out one other place first—the Uni-Mart on the corner of North Main and Hallan Avenue. Two minutes sooner and it would have been routine patrol as usual. Two minutes later and it would have been a report and an all-cars alert. Funny, Williams pondered later, how sometimes just a minute or two changed the world, at least that part of it you occupied.

A minute or two. It could kill you.

Although the night breezes still nipped exposed ears, it was May and not nearly cold enough for the ski mask and black trench coat worn by the tall black man in front of the convenience store. He had the store manager pressed back against the plate glass windows outside. Even from down the block, the officers were struck by the manager's paleness. The short, fat man's expression said Frankenstein had him by the scruff of the neck. His gaze darted, then locked onto the approaching patrol car.

Williams gassed his blue cruiser. As he whipped onto the parking lot, the masked man's head swiveled. He did a little jump back, then bolted around the end of the store like a cur-chased cat. The trembling manager pointed.

"Help! He was robbing me."

Williams and the lieutenant abandoned their car on the run. "Go inside the store and lock the door," Williams hurled back over his shoulder.

Because he hadn't seen a gun, Williams presumed the crime had been a strong-arm robbery. Some punk muscling the frightened storekeep into opening the cash register.

In this business you never assumed anything.

The alley behind the store split into two dark tunnels. Lieutenant Cochran turned right. Williams peeled off left, every sense suddenly awake. Cops lived for the bad guys-good guys chase. Adrenaline pumping, quarry just ahead, it was the reward for hours and hours of boredom.

Store buildings robbed the narrow alleyway of all light from Main Street. Williams proceeded cautiously north, searching. His flashlight beam stabbed the blackness, picking out dipsy Dumpsters and trash cans and the backyards of houses.

A shuffling sound to the right caught his attention. He turned, crouching. His flashlight beam exploded against the black guy sneaking alongside a house, like a fox trying to escape the farmer whose chicken house he had just raided. The thief's red mask, caught in the light, lent an absurd, surrealistic quality to the image.

"Police! Stand right there!" Williams ordered.

Not likely. The suspect took off like scalding water had been dashed at him.

"Shit!"

Up the alley, running hard. Williams kept himself in good physical condition, but he always said he was built for strength, not speed. His arms pumped and his breath whistled as he panted into his walkie-talkie, advising dispatch of developments. The light bar from the shining flashlight in his other hand bounced erratically, stabbing and goading the night.

The suspect had more incentive for speed. The lion merely runs for its supper; the gazelle runs for its life.

The policeman pounded along, keeping his prey's flitting shadow in sight. After initially losing ground, he began making up for it.

At the intersection of the alley with Katherine

Avenue, the fugitive circled the block and darted between two houses. The policeman was right behind him as he emerged into a backyard where trees leached away most of the moonlight. He ran into a tall picket fence, hunted frantically for a gate.

"Halt!"

Everything froze.

"Just stand right there."

Williams advanced toward the thief, who edged off along the fenceline. They paralleled each other, moving slowly and bristling like two dogs checking each other out before a fight. Officer Williams still had not gone for his service revolver; the police academy stressed to draw it only as a last resort. Twice Williams ordered the cornered man to surrender. Then he slipped his PR-24, a long, side-handled baton, from its ring.

Even on ski slopes, there was something almost sinister about a man wearing a ski mask. The sinister effect magnified itself here in this dark and lonely place.

The suspect's left hand snaked into his pocket and came out with what Williams assumed to be a knife. Popping the man hard on the wrist with his stick, sending the object flying, the husky cop pressed his advantage. He body-slammed the man to the ground and reached for his handcuffs.

Quick as a goosed hound, the bandit rolled and bounced to his feet. In his hand gleamed the object the policeman had knocked to the ground—a gun, glinting dully in a streak of pale moonlight penetrating the foliage.

Williams experienced a jolt of adrenaline. It was like his veins had been blasted with pure energy. He sprang at his opponent out of sheer desperation, his body wired for animal survival. The two men closed, grappled over the gun, trampled grass as they struggled across the lawn and crashed into the back of a garage.

The policeman concentrated on the suspect's gun hand. Williams banged it against a length of angle iron nailed to the garage wall. While the masked man felt exceptionally thin, he proved to be wiry and as strong and savage as a cornered puma.

The thought that he was fighting for his life filled Williams's brain. Fear surrounded him like a sweaty blanket.

The robber twisted free. He leaped back in a squat, and as he did he shoved the pistol straight out in front of him. Williams froze against the garage wall. Any movement now might excite the guy into squeezing the trigger.

"You don't want to do this, man," the officer reasoned, fighting to keep his voice from thinning into a shriek of terror. Few men know the feeling of looking down a gun barrel and seeing eternity at the other end.

Officer Dallas Williams knew—he *knew*—he was a dead man when he heard the snick of the hammer cocking.

"Draw against a drawn gun and you're a dead man," police firearms instructors lectured. "But if you're a dead man anyhow, go for it. Go down fighting."

Williams went for his gun.

Twin poppings from the bandit's .22-caliber Saturday night special! Flames stabbed the darkness.

The first bullet struck Williams's bulletproof vest, knocking him back against the garage. The second stung his upper right arm. A burst of pain, followed by instant numbness. He almost dropped his half-drawn weapon, but held onto it through a combination of luck and sheer stubbornness.

Payback!

Williams fired twice, from the hip, unable to lift his own gun any higher. The .38 roared heavier and throatier than the .22.

Standard training called for ripping off two shots, then pausing to judge their effects. The effects were instantaneous. The bandit, gut shot, dropped where he stood. He lay in a dark pile, gasping for breath. Williams's ears rang from the four shots all fired within a span of less than two seconds. Muzzle flashes burned on his retinas obscured his vision.

He was amazed at how quickly everything had happened.

"Officer needs help!" he radioed. His flashlight was gone, but the radio remained on his belt. "I'm shot—and the suspect is down!"

POSTSCRIPT: Officer Dallas Williams stood in the darkness clutching his wound and keeping the fallen bandit covered when backup cars and ambulances arrived. As soon as it was over, he began to tremble as though raw nerves were attached to voltage. He trembled for a long time afterward.

The bulletproof vest he wore likely saved him from more serious injury, even death. He soon recovered from the bullet wound to his arm and returned to duty.

The suspect, a forty-year-old ex-convict, survived two abdomen wounds and was subsequently sentenced to a term of five to fifteen years in the state penitentiary for armed robbery and shooting with intent to kill. He will most likely receive parole within five years.

13

A "Second Chance": The Bulletproof Vest

More than two thousand American police officers would likely be dead today but for the mugging of a Detroit pizza man in 1968.

Detroit, known as the "Murder Capital of the World," had a crime rate exceeded only by such other violent cities as Miami and sections of New York. Crime had become a national epidemic. Americans barred themselves inside their houses, hiding behind fences, guard dogs, and intruder alarms. For public businesses like convenience stores and fast-food restaurants, robbery and mugging became part of the overhead of doing business.

A young man named Richard Davis ran a pizzeria in downtown Detroit. His girlfriend—now his wife—helped with deliveries. One night a man telephoned in an order for two pepperoni-and-hams and gave an address in a rough sector of the city.

When Davis's girlfriend arrived with the delivery, she discovered the house blacked out. Three young men armed with handguns sprang from the bushes and robbed her of the pizzas and about thirty dollars. Heisting delivery people was a common sport.

A few nights later, a man again called in an order for two pepperoni-and-hams and gave an address suspiciously near where the previous robbery occurred. Davis decided to take the delivery himself. He couldn't afford to hire armed escorts, and the police were already too busy to concern themselves with a few penny-ante stickups. Armed citizens defending themselves was the only answer.

He slipped a six-shot .22-caliber revolver into the waistband of his trousers, packaged the pizzas, and found his way to the address. It was a house shoved among trees and bushes at the back end of the lot. Lots of places for muggers to hide. Davis looked around before he got out of his car. Seeing nothing unusual, he started toward the house. He kept his right hand free and near the butt of his little revolver.

His suspicions proved grounded. He was halfway to the door when three men leaped from the shadows with ready pistols in their fists. They surrounded him, brandishing their firepower.

"We be wantin' all your money, man. Just give it up, won't be no trouble."

"This time you ain't getting it," Davis shouted. He tossed the pizza aside and went for the RG-22 in his waistband.

Little .22s started popping like firecrackers. Tiny gun muzzles belched fireflies. The surprised thieves jumped around like grasshoppers on a stove, cussing and screaming and cracking shots at the pizza man.

Davis blasted one robber in the face; the dude screamed, clutched his eyes, and bolted. Davis took out a second one, who also grabbed himself and ran. The third one didn't have the guts to carry on the fight. It was a clear rout.

But the pizza man had not escaped unscathed.

Blood trickled from a bullet hole in his left leg. A bullet had also smashed his eyeglasses and cut a gory swath across his right cheekbone and temple.

"God bless the Saturday night special [small-caliber cheap handgun]," he quipped later. "I'd be dead now if they'd shot me with large-caliber pieces. Legislators are stupid. By outlawing Saturday night specials, they may as well pass laws saying all criminals have to carry big serviceable revolvers that *are* going to kill you. Besides, antigun laws are a lot like trying to stop a Nazi Panzer division with 'Keep Off Grass' signs."

Even if his wounds were small-caliber, Davis realized he may have been a bit foolish in forcing the confrontation. The thieves might have killed him and left his body in the darkness among empty pizza cartons. With the realization that he had faced real death came the germ of an idea that was to ultimately sweep the law enforcement community.

How, he wondered, could he protect his employees from such violent encounters? How could he, in essence, give them a *second chance* if they were robbed and shot? Maybe a bulletproof jumpsuit or shirt. He had never heard of such a thing, but surely the police had them. Police often thrust themselves into dangerous situations.

To his surprise, he soon learned that the best police departments offered were heavy metal-plated flak vests like those used by combat soldiers in Vietnam. Officers going on raids with the unwieldy armor charged ahead with some sense of security as they rushed armed and barricaded suspects.

There was only one problem. Virtually no police officer was slain when he knew in advance of the danger and prepared for it. Policemen died in "little Pearl Harbors"—surprise encounters while engaged in routine police work making traffic stops, settling domestic disputes, answering burglar alarms. Like pizza deliverymen threatened by muggers, policemen needed protection *all the time*. Something like a concealable garment light enough and comfortable enough to wear as normally as you wore underwear or T-shirts. A miracle shirt that bounced off bullets.

A Superman costume.

"It'll never work," he was advised. "Even if it is possible to devise a fabric bullets won't penetrate, the impact of the gunshot would still kill the wearer. It's like letting an Olympic weight lifter take a sledgehammer and pound you in the chest with it. The blow would break bones and crush organs and drive your ribs through your heart and lungs."

Davis still couldn't give up the idea. Feeling apprehensive and vulnerable because of what could have been his fatal encounter with criminals, he continued dreaming of a lightweight "second chance" bulletproof garment that could either be worn as a regular shirt or concealed underneath a regular shirt. People kept telling him it was a foolish idea—but then people had called Orville and Wilbur Wright foolish for wanting to fly.

In 1971 eight American police officers were shot to death over a single weekend. President Richard Nixon called FBI Director J. Edgar Hoover and asked, "What can we do about it?" The outcome was predictable—a lot of political windbagging and *nothing* done.

Davis knew the answer. The dead officers would still be alive if they had been wearing bulletproof shirts. The police deaths proved to be a catalyst for the pizza man's vision. A Superman suit *was* possible.

A true entrepreneur, Davis never went into anything halfway. He sold his pizzeria, oddly enough, to another amateur inventor named Robert Kearns who later invented the intermittent windshield wiper, and threw himself into experimenting with bulletproof materials.

He invested seventy dollars in a roll of ballistics nylon, the strongest, lightest fabric around. It wasn't much of an investment—but Walt Disney had started with only twenty six dollars. He cross-layered the nylon and shot it with .22s and .38s and 9mms, adding layer after layer until it reached 19-ply and stopped anything he fired at it.

Cutting and sewing, he shaped out a rough-looking vest consisting of the nineteen layers of ballistics nylon. It wasn't exactly Saks stylish, but it was reasonably pliable and only a fraction of the weight and bulk of the flak jackets currently used by police.

There remained one major question. The vest stopped bullets, true, but would the gunshot impact still kill?

There was only one way to find out.

Working on the assumption that the vest would spread the bullet's impact to its entire surface and thereby reduce the shock, Davis called an ambulance, just in case he was wrong, and prepared to shoot himself. He draped the vest over his thigh, then shot it with a hot .38 load.

The bullet left him with an ugly black and green bruise, but the ordeal wasn't the horrible thing he had been warned against. It broke no bones and caused relatively little tissue damage. He hobbled around on the leg, displaying it like a medal.

The vest *would* provide its wearer a second chance.

But he still had to go further—to make sure.

"You're crazy!" his wife warned. "That's enough. Please?"

"How can the police officers and others trust my armor if I don't trust it myself?" he argued.

After all, Wilbur and Orville took the risks first by flying their own airplane.

Davis again alerted ambulances and donned the vest. He pressed the muzzle of a .38 pistol against his own chest and squeezed the trigger. The impact staggered him, but the vest caught the bullet and his resulting wound proved even less severe than when he shot himself in the thigh. He was elated. A dream had become a reality.

Today, in testing and perfecting his armor, Richard Davis has survived more gunshots than any other man in the world, having been shot or having shot himself somewhere around 140 times.

In late 1972, the Second Chance Body Armor Company went into production, operating out of Davis's house in Detroit with neighbors hired to do the stitching. Orders soon backlogged as word spread to police departments across the nation. More orders poured in every time the armor saved another policeman's life.

Officer Ronald Jagielski of the Detroit police department was Davis's first recorded gunshot "save." Weeks after Second Chance went into production, Jagielski wore a vest when he and several other narcs surrounded a dopers' pad and moved in for the raid. Just as he approached the house, a shot penetrated the door and hit him in the chest. He later found the .38-caliber slug imbedded in his vest. His only injury was a small bruise.

The lives of two other policemen were saved by the vest the first day they wore them. Illinois State Trooper Kim Rhoades survived after she was shot multiple times in the chest during what started out as a routine traffic arrest. Another policeman walked away after being blasted by a 12-gauge shotgun firing a rifled slug. A rifled slug will bust a car engine.

Davis's continuing experiments and the development of space-age materials such as Kevlar have permitted him to perfect a bulletproof vest that, today, is not much heavier than a shirt and almost as comfortable. No lives are saved, he believes, unless the armor is comfortable enough to wear all the time. A policeman never knows when he may need it.

To date, Second Chance has sold more than three hundred thousand vests. Most of them were bought by police officers, although Special Operations Forces also used them during the Desert Storm war in Iraq. Following Davis's success, a number of other companies began manufacturing lightweight body armor. Second Chance and the other two or three leading companies in the field claim a total of more than two thousand police "saves" since the mid-1970s.

Davis published a booklet which lists chronologically the 528 to-date "saves" attributed to the wearing of Second Chance bulletproof vests. Incident after incident, it is testimony to the violence that rules the streets of American cities—and a kind of monument to the dreams of a pizza man who would give victims of criminal gunfire a second chance at life. . . .

Motorcycle Officer Bob Hooper, San Francisco. He stopped a motorist on a routine traffic violation. The violator pulled a gun and shot Hooper in the chest. His vest saved his life.

Officer Randy Mullens, Houston, Texas. Shot by a burglar exiting a house with a stolen TV in one hand and a .25-caliber semiautomatic pistol in the other. Saved by his vest.

Officer John Zipperner, Jacksonville, Florida. Hit twice by a "loiterer" firing a .38. His armor caught both bullets.

Officer Steve Snyder, Lima, Ohio. He was hit four times in an exchange of gunfire with an armed robbery suspect. So was his assailant. The assailant was not wearing a bulletproof vest.

The list continues, a tribute from live policemen who might otherwise have been dead statistics. Yet, not all incidents ended so successfully. Wearing a "Superman suit" is not certain insurance against criminal violence.

For example, a robbery suspect shot a police officer four times in the vest with a .45-caliber pistol. The policeman returned fire, bringing his assailant down. The dying gunman got off one last round that struck the officer in the lower intestine below the vest, killing him instantly.

A California policeman survived one shooting, saved by his vest, only to die four years later when a criminal shot him in the head. He was wearing his vest at the time.

Still another lawman died in an on-duty automobile accident one month after his vest saved his life from gunfire.

On one heartbreaking occasion, a policeman's wife ordered a vest as a surprise for her crime fighting mate. Second Chance shipped the armor the day after it received the order; Davis insists that orders be mailed immediately. That same night, the unprotected policeman died in a shoot-out. His vest arrived the next day.

Many police departments, recognizing the advantages of its policemen wearing armor, today issue bulletproof vests as routinely as they issue uniforms and handguns. While the police death toll in America's continuing war against street crime remains the highest of any civilized country, it would be much higher if pizza man Richard Davis's mugging had not inspired him to consider the possibilities of a "Superman" shirt that would literally provide gunfire victims a second chance to live.

14

Officer Stacey Collins, Littleton, Colorado

October 2, 1986, 1:19 A.M.

In Denver to the north, a cop could count on action about any night of the week, twenty-four hours a day. Littleton, a Denver suburb, was a bit tamer. It was a bedroom community. People came home at the end of a workday and went to bed. The middle of a week was almost always slow. The police department fielded six or eight cars at the most, to protect a permanent population of about thirty-five thousand.

Stacey Collins, a tall athletic rookie policeman at six-feet-three and 215 pounds, went on Thursday shift at midnight to celebrate his first year's anniversary on the department. One year was a breaking point; a rookie went off probation and was no longer considered a rookie.

Young and eager—catching a burglar was always good for a boost of adrenaline—Collins ran his district once, quickly, nosing the white-and-orange scout car down the alleys off Bowles and South Federal looking for business breaks. Satisfied that there were no break-ins or burglar alarms going off to

115

embarrass him if the sergeant should check, he cut back toward Bowles beneath a cold October mountain sky filled with stars.

Bowles Avenue was the main drag through Littleton. It was heavily commercial with mom-and-pop shops, small businesses, the usual tourist stuff. The teenage drive-ins and video arcades had locked their doors before midnight, leaving only two young lovers wrapped up like octopi advancing slowly along the sidewalk. The girl waved. Collins grinned and waved back.

Traffic was light at one A.M. The bars were closing, drunks stumbling out to load their vehicles like loading cartridges into a .38 and thumbing back the hammer.

"I *had* to drive, Officer. I was too drunk to walk."

The policeman pulled into the semidarkened parking lot of a closed fast-food joint and parked, headlights doused, engine running. He sat there observing traffic for the telltale signs of a DUI, a drunk driver—weaving, speeding, or driving too slowly, sudden starts and stops . . .

He unconsciously adjusted the bulletproof vest worn underneath his navy blue uniform shirt. Vests were not standard issue with the Littleton police department, but Dan McCaskey, a patrolman friend in nearby Lakewood, had loaned it to Collins. That was three weeks ago. Collins still found it uncomfortable. He didn't have a wife to remind him to put it on nights before a shift and might have discarded it but for McCaskey.

"Wear it, you'll get used to it," McCaskey insisted. "In this business you never know when it might save your ass."

In the back of his mind, Collins realized policemen *were* shot and killed, but he never thought it would happen to him. When you were twenty three years old, life was all out there ahead of you. You felt immortal, invincible.

Collins glanced at his watch. His car radio remained as dead as a chunk of lava. Maybe he should have requested the night off, picked up a date, celebrated the end of his rookie year. More action than sitting here on the strip in the middle of the week watching the sidewalks fold up.

Honking attracted his attention. A Chevy swerved lanes to pass a slow-moving pickup truck. The orange rattletrap Ford with the missing tailgate chugged on past, heading east as carefully as a mouse passing a cat in the pantry. Creeping along like that was the same as hanging a sign on the bumper: *Take a Look at Me; I'm DUI.*

Collins flicked on his headlights and eased in behind the pickup. It caught the red light at Bowles and Santa Fe Drive and sat through a complete red and green cycle before gunning through the intersection on the next red. That did it. Collins lit up his red-and-blue light bar like a marquee.

The truck pulled over immediately, jumping the curb in front of a row of night-lighted businesses, all closed. Collins stopped behind with his car pulled out into the lane a little to provide a protection envelope. Flashlight in hand, he approached the driver. His height gave him an unobstructed view through the open pickup window to where the elderly white male sat quietly behind the wheel staring straight ahead. He was slender, white-haired, and wore glasses. One of the old farmers from down in the valley. Somebody's grandpa who had gone out and latched onto a snootful.

"Sir, may I see your driver's license and registration? The reason I stopped you is because you just ran the red light."

The old man said nothing. His head slowly turned

until his glasses reflected the patrol car's rotating beacons. His expression remained calm, almost indifferent.

In the next instant his hand snapped up like the head of a rattler. It contained a tiny .25 semiautomatic. The gun barked, flung flames. Collins felt the bullet strike low on the left side of his bulletproof vest. It felt like he had been jabbed with a knitting needle. Surprise and the impact staggered him backward. The flashlight flew from his hand.

Every synapse in his brain short-circuited. Running on survival instinct, he sprinted low around the back of the pickup and took cover behind a thick oak growing on the median between the street and the sidewalk. Breathing hard from the sudden adrenaline push, he still maintained enough presence of mind to radio for a backup on his portable.

"Unit 141—I've been hit, shot in the stomach!"

A call like that—*cop shot!*—was enough to bring every policeman within hearing. Denver cops would be on the way. Almost immediately Collins heard the reassuring scream of distant sirens.

For all the hurry, the old man might have been about to plow his back forty. While Officer Collins watched, filled with shock and amazement, the grandpa casually opened his pickup truck door and slid onto the street. Zombielike, gun held low along his side, he started toward the policeman as though he intended to finish the job he had started. His eyes, fixated with purpose, were staring and large through the thick lenses of his glasses.

The old sonofabitch was crazy. He was at least sixty years old, thin, white-haired.

"Look, you stay back," Collins shouted. "Stop. Throw down the gun. I'm warning you. I'll shoot."

The grandpa's expression remained distinctly indifferent, like his body was there but his mind wasn't.

Collins pinned him against the sights of his .357. For all the excitement, even considering he might have been lying dead in the street if not for the borrowed vest, his hand remained surprisingly steady.

He didn't want to shoot the old bastard. But the old bastard just kept coming, crossing behind the pickup between it and the patrol car with its flashing lights. Collins's trigger finger tightened. He screamed at the grandpa to stop; he *pleaded* for him to stop.

The first backup car arrived, peeling rubber, light bar throbbing. Patrolman John Fangman had been just around the corner. As his cruiser slid to a stop, he flung open his door and took cover behind it, his revolver leveled on the violator.

The grandpa hesitated, distracted.

"Drop it, old man! Drop it!" Fangman yelled.

As the scene proceeded to play itself out in slow motion, the zombie paused in stalking the first policeman and slowly turned his head toward the second. His gun hand started up.

"Don't do it!" Fangman warned.

The .25 popped. The bullet ricocheted off Fangman's hood, whined toward the stars for what seemed an eternity, but which couldn't have been more than the time it took for police trigger fingers to tighten.

Four heavy-caliber gunshots crashed so closely together that they merged into a single prolonged explosion. Each cop fired twice. Through muzzle smoke and flame they saw the old man collapse to the pavement.

He never moved again on his own. His glasses and his gun lay next to him while blood pooled deep and thick around his thin body.

Collins the rookie who was no longer a rookie stayed frozen behind his tree, numbed by how suddenly it all developed. Perhaps two minutes had passed altogether, but it seemed like ages ago that he had flipped on his light bar to make the stop. It was a lifetime ago for the old man lying in the street.

He felt a hand on his shoulder, glanced around to see sergeant's stripes.

"Son, the man's down. You can go ahead and put your gun away."

POSTSCRIPT: Later, Stacey Collins learned that the violator had been previously convicted of vehicular manslaughter. The judge who convicted him promised to send him back to prison if he were ever caught DUI again. That was the only motive for what he did. He started carrying a gun just in case some cop stopped him. He wasn't going back to prison—and he wasn't going to quit drinking and driving. He would kill a cop first.

15

Officer Gene "Buddy" Evans, Arlington, Texas

February 26, 1988, 5:00 A.M.

All Officer Buddy Evans wanted that cold Texas February night was to help the lady. That was all he wanted—and look what happened.

He found out later she was a paranoid schizophrenic. People were out to get her. She had just been released for the fifth time from a mental institution. It was scary. There were a lot of people like her out there in a megalopolis like the Dallas–Fort Worth area. Because the little city of Arlington sat along the artery that fed back and forth between the two larger cities, it got everything Dallas got—robberies, homicides, vice.

It got everything.

Working graveyards, from midnight to seven A.M., didn't give Evans as much time as he wanted with his three-year-old daughter, but he liked the shift. With four years service on the Arlington police department, he wasn't exactly a rookie but he wasn't a veteran either. He still liked getting out there and mixing it up with the bad guys, prowling the nighttime streets searching for burglars and other miscreants. There was an old cop saying that went, *Nobody's on the streets after midnight except cops and thieves. If you ain't one, you have to be the other.*

Earlier in the day before the night shifts began, a heavyset brunette in her early thirties stopped at the police station. She wore a big smile as she carried in several bottles of Mountain Dew soda and left them with the desk sergeant. Dropping off treats wasn't common, but it wasn't so unusual either. Sports had its groupies; so did the police.

"Something for the boys in blue," chirped the visitor, cheerful and well dressed in dark slacks and a long-sleeved sweater. "Make sure everybody gets some. They deserve it, what with the job they do fighting crime and everything."

The woman had written a short letter to her husband and left it for him to find before she embarked on her mission. *Don't worry about me,* the letter began. *I'm going to kill a police officer tonight. They'll call you the next day and tell you what happened. . . .*

When she made her presentations to the desk sergeant, she wasn't exactly thinking of quenching thirsts. What she was thinking, it turned out, was something like, *When I shoot one of them I can watch the Mountain Dew spew out his chest.*

Crazy as she was, she shoved a Charter Arms .38-caliber revolver into her purse shortly after nightfall, climbed into her gray Subaru station wagon, and started hunting. Usually, it wasn't hard to find a cop.

She tried convenience stores and all-night eateries. No cops around. Several patrolling cruisers passed her, but she didn't think quickly enough to get one to stop. Finally, tired from driving around, she calculated the best way to get a cop was to set a trap using herself as bait.

By that time it was halfway into the graveyard shift

and heading for dawn. Traffic was exceptionally light on a cold, crisp night that kept even insomniacs inside off the streets. Insanely obsessed with her deadly mission, the woman stopped her car in a moving lane, turned off the ignition, and waited.

At the police station, Officer Evans finished booking a misdemeanor arrest. His breath made brittle balloons in the predawn air. Another hour and he'd be getting off-watch and going home to find a warm place next to his wife. He had time for another quick sweep around his district to make sure burglars hadn't carried it off, then coffee and rolls at the doughnut shop on Abram Street.

It was the winter quiet time in the morning before traffic rush began. Evans always liked the city at this time of morning; the streets were all his except for the normal routine—a street sweeper huffing along like a giant beetle, the Dallas *Herald* newspaper truck dumping bundles onto a parking lot.

Hazard lights flashing at the intersection of Abram and Collins was not part of the normal routine. Evans cruised up behind the stalled Subaru station wagon, flipping on his overhead lights to ward off other traffic. The rotating beacons pulsated intermittent red against the head of a chunky brunette who sat on the passenger's side of the vehicle staring straight ahead. It appeared the car had run out of gas or something and the woman's husband had gone for help. What a miserable night for car trouble.

The officer radioed in a routine "Assist Motorist" before he got out of his car to walk up to the driver's side of the Subaru. The cold morning air bit at him even through his coat, his long handles, and the ballistics vest he wore underneath his khakis. He tapped on the driver's window with his flashlight.

"Ma'am, what seems to be the problem?"

The car heater was going inside and he couldn't

understand her reply. She reached to roll down the window, but she was rather large and seemed to be having difficulty. It wasn't that she was drunk.

"Hold on a minute. I'll come around to your side."

She rolled down her window as the officer strolled around the back of the station wagon and approached her. Her head came out the open window wearing a strange, hollow smile. Only the lips moved. It gave Evans a start of the sort experienced when a Texas rattler appears unexpectedly.

Right behind the smile appeared the pistol. The pistol flashed.

It happened that suddenly. No warning. Nothing. Just that crazy smile and the report of the weapon loud and hard in the frozen air. Evans felt the bulletproof vest pop against his chest as the .38 slug struck centerline.

His brain automatically associated getting shot with getting dead. He forgot all about the vest. He thought he was dying. Disbelief and shock overloaded his electrical circuits. Pictures of his wife and child raced through his jumbled thoughts.

All I wanted to do was help her.

While his brain short-circuited, his body operated on survival mode and training. Driven back by a combination of bullet impact and startled reaction, he whipped out his service revolver and fired two quick shots through the station wagon's back window. Glass exploded in his face.

He crouched behind the Subaru and shouted into his hand radio: *"10-33! 10-33! Officer in shooting! I've been shot once, and I'm shooting at the suspect."*

He stuck his head up and threw two more quick shots through the window. The windshield went crashing onto the hood.

He hesitated.

The woman remained sitting on the passenger's seat

as unperturbed as though she were watching *Dirty Harry* at the movies, like she was still waiting for her husband to return with help. Shards of glass picked up light from the Western Auto on one corner and the hamburger joint across the street and filled her dark hair with sparkles.

She sat there, unmoving.

Evans blinked.

The lady had just shot a cop—and she was just sitting there.

The other cops would rib him about this one for years afterward: "Evans, you *killed* her car all around her. She sat there and let you shoot at her—and you didn't even muss her perm."

Cops were like that, afterward.

Evans wouldn't miss again. He centered the front sighting post of his weapon directly on the back of her head. A stationary target. No glass remained in the back window to deflect *this* bullet.

The target remained perfectly motionless.

"Lady," the policeman yelled. "Throw out the gun or I'll kill you. Throw it out. Now!"

She did, moving slowly. Evans saw her face. She looked dumfounded, probably because her bullet hadn't killed the cop as she intended. But apparently she didn't have the heart to try it again. The .38 revolver clunked as it struck the pavement.

Officer Evans had the fat woman handcuffed in the street and was sitting on her for good measure when the first backup arrived. She still hadn't uttered a word. She didn't start talking until she reached the station house where she complained to detectives that Evans had shot at her. It outraged her.

"That policeman was trying to kill me," she cried. "He was trying to shoot me. Don't tell me he wasn't. I know he was out to get me."

"It's not paranoia," a detective said, laughing, "if somebody really *is* trying to shoot you."

POSTSCRIPT: Officer Buddy Evans suffered a painful bruise where the .38-caliber bullet struck his ballistics vest, but he was back to work within three days patrolling the midnight shift.

16

Narc Officer Dwight Stalls II, Newport News, Virginia

September 28, 1987, 11:00 P.M.

Working an informant, a snitch, is a delicate affair. Defense attorneys always make a big deal of informants being criminals themselves and therefore untrustworthy. The criminal part is true. Most snitches are criminals. The good ones are. Who else but street punks know enough about other criminals to snitch on them?

Cops simply use criminals against each other. That's the way it is. Say a policeman catches some dude up tight on a nickel-and-dime deal that the courts will let him off on anyhow. He cuts the dude a little slack in exchange for some good information. The policeman owns the dude from then on. He wants something, he goes to his snitch. Find out this, find out that. Who's dealing, and how.

An odd kind of relationship builds up between the two. It even gets where the dude *likes* working for the police to fuck over other street people. He gets his kicks playing cops-and-robbers on the cop's side of the fence for a change. It gives him a sense of power or something.

Who could figure it?

Police Narcs Dwight Stalls and his partner R. F. Dawes gave their snitch a quick look as they cruised a block on Roanoke Avenue. The snitch—call him Boogie—pointed to a two-story cream-yellow house set back from the street among a few ill-kept trees.

"That be the baby right there," Boogie said, sticking his head up to window level in the backseat of the undercover car, then ducking down again.

If the occupants of the house saw him, a black dude, with two white guys, they'd figure him for a snitch right off. A snitch's life among dopers had less value than a used syringe.

The neighborhood was bursting open with dope. The government projects—Dickerson Court, Newsome Park, Seven Oaks—bred dope and dopers. Dudes in pimp trousers and Raebocks stood out front of the projects and dealt crack like used car salesmen.

Newport News itself was bursting open with dope. Sometimes narcs felt half the city's 150,000 population was either dealing or using. The night glow over Chesapeake Bay wasn't from the lights of Norfolk, Virginia Beach, Portsmouth, and Newport News; it came from all the dopers getting their nightly glow-on. If somebody seized all the dope from the area and dumped it into the Chesapeake River, pols in D.C. would be getting high off the mist.

Maybe the pols *were* getting high off it. Maybe that was what was wrong with the government.

Boogie was what the courts termed a *reliable* informant. That meant the information he gave police had been tested in court and found dependable. Stalls and Dawes had used him before in making controlled buys.

This was going to be another one. Boogie said two guys living at the Roanoke address dealt coke. One was called "Mac." He didn't know the other guy.

Dawes frisked the snitch to make sure he didn't have any dope on him. Lawyers were always bringing that up as a defense, that the snitch had the shit on him before he made the alleged buy. Then the policemen gave the skinny black man, an addict himself, one hundred dollars in bills marked for evidence to prove an exchange was made.

"Get what you can get—a gram of nose or some crack—whatever," Stalls coached the informant. "No grass. We don't want any marijuana."

It was hard enough to convict on coke. Judges laughed at policemen who brought grass busts into their courtrooms, grass was so common. Another few years and they'd be laughing out coke arrests. To narcs, it was a fucked-up world. They did their job, what they thought was right. Who could figure that nobody really gave a damn! Dopers were the real lowlife of the criminal world. Cops trusted killers more than they trusted dopers.

Boogie disappeared with the hundred dollars in bills into the dopers' pad while the two undercover narcs waited, slunk low in their car. Anybody noticing them would likely have paid little attention anyhow. Stalls was youngish, in his twenties, and wore his brown hair long to match a short beard. Dawes was older, already with twenty years on the department and about to retire. Gray flecked his scruffy hair; he had earned the lines in his face the hard way, dealing with street scum for so many years.

Stalls always figured he'd look like his partner some day—hard, cynical, capable. Old cops had that look, like they had seen it all and nothing would ever surprise them again.

"He's coming out," Dawes murmured, nodding.

Boogie gave a subtle signal from the porch and walked down the street. The narcs waited until he was out of sight of the house, then picked him up. He forked over about a gram of white powder—coke, nose candy. Stalls grinned.

"You did good, Boogie."

"Boogie always do good," Boogie said.

It was a good case, so far. "Yessir, Your Honor. The informant was clean when he went inside the house. We had him under constant surveillance when he went in, and again when he came out. The only place he could have picked up the substance was inside the house."

Two hours later the narcs had their search warrant. By then it was about an hour short of midnight. It was early fall, September, but ice already laced the breezes sifting in off the Chesapeake. Stalls stuffed his stainless steel S&W Model 60 into his trouser belt and pulled his light windbreaker closed against the chill. He and a little army of six other narcs parked their cars down the block from the Roanoke house. Shadows flitted as they surrounded the place. Two narcs took the back door, two others crouched in the shadows to watch the side windows on either side. Dawes, Stalls, and a husky black narc named J. T. Henderson slipped to the front door.

A raid was like turning on the lights in a filthy kitchen. Hypes, junkies, and pushers scurried in and out of every crack, like cockroaches.

Henderson played decoy at the front door, while the two white cops flattened themselves against the darkened wall out of sight. If "Mac" peeped out and saw a black guy, he'd probably open the door. If he spotted a honky, everything in the house except the sofa went down the toilet stool.

J.T. knuckled the door. Stalls crouched in the shotgun slot, ready to enter first. He had his badge in his left hand and his revolver in his right.

Like most cops, Stalls liked raids—the tension beforehand, the anticipation of a major score, the gut ripping excitement of busting into unknown territory where you never knew what might happen. Narcs and dopers was the game played at its pinnacle.

The door eased open about a foot, framing a typical doper type with ratty nappy hair. A dim orange glow from behind silhouetted his head and shoulders. He wore a multicolor silk pullover shirt and black pants. Pushers, like pimps, went first class.

"Yeah, man, whattya want?" the dude asked.

Mac was the code word that opened the door.

"Let me talk to Mike," J.T. said.

Jesus. Stalls caught his breath. *Mac.* Not *Mike.* Pushers were so goddamned paranoid they wouldn't let their own mothers in if everything wasn't right.

Stalls recognized the wary expression that crossed the pusher's dark features. Everything was starting to go down wrong. Before the door could slam in Henderson's face, Stalls jumped into view with his badge stuck out in front of him and the Model 60 posed at his hip. Adrenaline started coursing in his veins.

"Police officer!" he shouted.

The way things were supposed to work was J.T. kicked the door wide and Stalls rushed in followed by the others. Only, it didn't quite go down like that. Stalls had always heard about slow-motion time when you got your short hairs caught up tight. The next instants passed like that, like in a nightmare when you're trying to run from the monster and all you can do is take one long, slow, agonizing step at a time.

Stalls watched the dealer's left hand go down,

131

down, down. It came back up in the same slow motion, this time filled with a black revolver. The two men stood so near each other that Stalls felt the guy's breath. The gun pressed into his chest and fired.

It was like a camera flash going off, but instead of white light it was the same orange light that burned inside the house. The cop experienced a firm jolt, like someone had suddenly pounded him in the ribs with the palm of his hand.

He returned fire, squeezing off four shots to make the orange camera flash go off in rapid sequence. At point-blank range he hit the gunman twice—once in the forearm and once in the thigh—and missed him twice.

Stalls was a good shot on the range. He was close enough to his target that he could have reached out and slapped him on the head with the gun barrel. Yet, he missed *twice*.

The doper fell to the floor screaming like he was being murdered. Stalls suffered only a terrific bruise to the sternum. His bulletproof vest caught the bullet and saved his life.

POSTSCRIPT: A lenient judge sentenced the dope dealer to eight years in the penitentiary for shooting the narc. Stalls always wondered how much time the guy would have received for murder if he hadn't been wearing the vest.

The only things the narcs recovered from the pad were residue and some glassine bags. "Mac" had disappeared, leaving his unsuspecting henchman behind to receive cops he obviously expected. Stalls always believed Mac was tipped off by a female police officer passing information to her cousin in the streets.

Snitches. You had snitches on both sides.

Four months after Stalls was shot, Narcotics Officer J. T. Henderson made another raid and was himself shot twice in the chest with a .32-caliber revolver. Like Stalls, he wore a bulletproof vest and survived with only a few bruises to show for his ordeal.

17

Special Weapons and Tactics

In 1974 the American public received its introduction to the first specialized unit in the United States created for the calculated, deliberate, and controlled use of deadly force. Terrorists calling themselves the Symbionese Liberation Army died inside their flaming hideout fighting against deadly looking police officers dressed in black jumpsuits and gas masks and armed with sniper rifles and automatic weapons. The debut of SWAT (Special Weapons and Tactics) signaled the beginning of a new era in society's war against escalating violence.

The concept of a police "Special Forces" had grown slowly but steadily during the last years of the turbulent sixties and into the decade of the 1970s. The year before the SLA shoot-out, three terrorists commandeered the downtown Howard Johnson Hotel in New Orleans and opened fire on pedestrians and police. The shoot-out continued for more than thirty hours, until the heavily armed snipers were finally driven to the hotel roof where police in Marine combat helicopters raked them with machine gun fire.

Unlike Los Angeles, New Orleans had no "Special Forces." The firefight claimed three dead cops, five wounded, and the deaths and injuries of several firemen and civilians.

The New Orleans hotel battle, the Los Angeles SLA shoot-out, and the 1973 slaying of athletes at the Munich Olympic games suddenly made SWAT the most fashionable—and perhaps necessary—trend to sweep law enforcement since the advent of radio patrol cars. Police departments across the nation, including the New Orleans police, shot inquiries to Chief Darryl Gates in Los Angeles inquiring about the training and deployment of his SWAT teams. Demands increased dramatically for SWAT training offered by the FBI at its Quantico, Virginia, bureau.

Chief Gates devised the Los Angeles SWAT in 1967 in the aftermath of the Watts rioting during which snipers and barricaded gunmen shot it out with policemen in mini-firefights. The spark for the creation, he said, was the increasingly maniac nature of modern urban crime—riots, hijackings, bank robberies with hostages, armed mental patients barricading themselves inside buildings, and mad killers opening fire on complete strangers.

"Probably every major city needs something to deal with the strange kinds of situations that develop," Gates said.

In forming their "special actions" teams, cities viewed the threat from different perspectives. Sergeant Robert Ingbrittsen of the Daly City, California, police department said the main reason for the formation of his SWAT was "to combat the new type of warfare put on by militant groups." St. Louis and Boston responded to racial disturbances; Washington and Minneapolis were at least partly motivated by antiwar and civil rights demonstrations coupled with political crimes and terrorist attacks.

Even small towns got caught up in the craze. Tiny Hillsborough, California, trained a two-man team, while Shelly, Idaho, population 1,600, built a six-man team using virtually its entire department. SWAT with its military overtones and its training to employ violence against violence had become a permanent fixture of the police community.

"This is a day of specialization," said former Atlanta Mayor Sam Massell who approved his city's creation of a SWAT team. "That's what SWAT is all about—a group of experts."

The essential strategy of SWAT is built around the concept of a team, normally five men, whose expertise is primarily in heavy firepower. Many specially selected SWAT officers have military infantry experience. Additional police training in urban tactics and firearms make them formidable in the use of M16 rifles, semiautomatic pistols, tear gas guns, sniper rifles, and even light machine guns and explosives.

The teams are broken down into areas of function —entry and rescue, containment and arrest, sniper and observer. Many departments have now added hostage negotiators and even psychologists to their teams.

All SWAT men are regular police officers who undergo additional training and carry around tactical gear in the trunks of their patrol cars. They work regular street shifts, called into action as a team only when a situation develops that requires their special talents. Law enforcement officials quickly deny that SWAT men are trained killers.

"Our purpose is to save lives," SWAT commanders insist.

Until the SLA shoot-out, the Los Angeles police

department's SWAT had killed only one other person in its seven-year history. The Tulsa, Oklahoma SOT (Special Operations Team) had fired only three shots during more than three hundred callouts over a ten-year period. One of the shots was an accidental discharge; the other two resulted in suspect fatalities. Most city SWAT teams have never killed anyone.

"The whole training philosophy is that we're not successful if we cause damage to anyone," explained Chief Gates. "We would consider that to be a failure if we harmed someone."

The SLA shoot-out, he said, was a failure for that reason.

Suggested Swat Procedures

(Developed by the National Tactical Officers Association)

1. SWAT commanders are informed of a situation that demands special tactics. They alert SWAT members and hostage negotiators.
2. Officers establish an inner perimeter to contain the suspect and isolate the site. The ranking SWAT officer assumes command pending arrival of supervisors.
3. As more officers respond, they are assigned to an outer perimeter for traffic and crowd control. Fire engines and radio cars block streets and intersections.
4. Supervisors establish locations for a command post, along with facilities, sites, and avenues for emergency services.
5. All SWAT members are briefed on the situation and kept informed of developments. Marksmen (long rifle snipers) are placed into position to protect scouts.

6. Hostage negotiators attempt to contact the suspect by telephone. A PA announcement may be used in conjunction with the telephone.

7. Operations commanders and department executives make a tentative plan based upon information obtained by scouts.

8. SWAT teams are briefed on the plan and their role in it. They are assigned their functions as arrest teams, entry teams, security teams, etc. The command post plots positions on a diagram and maintains a chronological log of events.

9. Team members deploy to their predesignated positions.

10. If an impasse is reached with the suspect, advise him tear gas will be used if he does not surrender. (Only with an armed suspect who does not have a hostage.)

11. A specific amount of tear gas is fired or launched on command into specific locations.

12. Negotiators keep the suspect's phone ringing after gas is introduced so he is able to receive immediate surrender instructions.

13. If suspect still refuses to surrender, SWAT entry teams are launched to go in after him.

14. If the suspect holds a hostage, one entry team rehearses rescue procedures using a mock-up of the actual location, while a second entry team assumes a position near the actual site in case it becomes necessary to make an immediate entry.

15. Use marksmen (snipers) if necessary to neutralize the suspect.

16. After the incident is concluded, supervisors assess damage to property and ensure all team members are accounted for. Participants submit their reports and are debriefed. Detectives conduct full investigation if shooting occurs.

18

Officer Bob Connolly, Milwaukee, Wisconsin

May 7, 1989, 7:15 A.M.

Sergeant William Skurzewski stood tall in a dark alley off North Martin Luther King Drive, in the downtown heart of Milwaukee, and selected Unit Five of the Police Tactical Enforcement Unit to accompany him to the roof. The coppers of the assault team milled nervously about as they waited heavily armed for the word to go. They looked rugged in dark blue coveralls, flak vests, and Marine soft caps.

Five men were on the team—Sergeant Skurzewski, team leader; Mark Koch on the bulletproof shield; Bob Connolly, cover man; Richard Wagner, armed with an H&K 9mm submachine gun; Rod Gustafson, a big man with a 20-pound sledgehammer and a heavy pry bar called a "Hooligan tool."

"Be ready," Skurzewski advised. "The asshole's not coming out."

The standoff began at about 3:00 A.M. when the man in the apartment on the roof started shooting up his place. A bullet penetrated the wall and dropped into bed with the lady in the apartment next door. She

140

heard more shots, then a violent quarrel between the gunman and his roommate. She took to her heels and telephoned police.

Nothing more had emanated from the apartment since police arrived. Just silence. Hour after hour. A police hostage negotiator on a bullhorn kept at it anyhow, his amplified voice futilely attempting to raise some response.

"He's either dead up there," a policeman predicted, "or he's sitting in there waiting for a target in blue."

Obviously the man wasn't coming out; the TAC team would have to go in to find out if he had murdered his roommate and committed suicide, or if he held his roommate hostage and was simply biding his time.

The guy's name, Sergeant Ski informed his men, was James R. Baker, white male, forty-eight, recently working on his third divorce. Deep state of depression. It was the profile of a man capable of destroying everything he could before destroying himself.

The sad sonofabitch.

Officer Bob Connolly in the alley studied the apartment on the roof while the sergeant briefed his team and sketched the layout using information gleaned from the lady who fled after the bullet landed in bed with her. The apartment resembled a fortified WWII German blockhouse placed squarely on the flat roof of a used-furniture store. Easily defended. It contained two apartments.

"A door opens onto the roof at the top of these stairs," the sergeant explained. "It's about twenty feet across the roof to the apartment door. We'll be in the open and exposed for a second or two. Inside the apartment building is a short hallway with two more doors on the right. The first door is the neighbor's, the second belongs to our suspect."

Police snipers had already slipped into positions on the roofs and floors of adjacent buildings. They reported shades drawn and no movement from the suspect's fortress.

The rising sun backlighted city skyscrapers with the promise of another lovely May morning. It picked out silhouettes of armed policemen who surrounded the building and contained the gunman within their perimeter. The alley below was full of uniforms.

This wouldn't be the first time Connolly had busted a gunman from his barricade. The years were starting to show in the lines etched on his face. Twenty years on the mean streets, the last twelve as a TAC member working high crime and taking on jobs like this where a copper could get his balls shot off.

He had wearily dragged his forty-three-year-old body out of the Sunday morning sack when the telephone awoke him for the callout alert. Sitting on the edge of the bed, shaking out the sleep cobwebs, he noticed how he had put on weight, thickened a little around the belt line. Middle age. Age, damn it. Age would kill you when nothing else did. Life itself was terminal.

His wife, Judy, was accustomed to his being called out in the middle of the night.

"Be careful, honey," she said.

"I'm always careful."

For some reason Connolly paused in front of his daughter's door on his way out. Carrie with a beautiful smile like her mother's. It brightened a room faster than a morning sun. How excited she had been at becoming a teenager. Connolly shrugged off the impulse to step quietly inside, watch her sleeping. Wearing a half-grin, he left the house and drove speeding to the callout site on Martin Luther King Drive.

Life had been good to him.

Life apparently had not been so good to James R. Baker on the roof of the furniture store.

By full daylight Baker had still not responded to entreaties from the hostage negotiator.

Sergeant Ski issued his warning order: "Unit Five, get ready. We don't know what we'll find up there. Be alert for a hostage."

Policemen were action-oriented. Tension dissipated as the movements started. A uniformed patrolman threw "thumbs-up" as the assault team took to the stairwell with a purpose and scurried to the roof. It staged briefly at the roof door. Each man took a deep breath, checked his equipment and weapons, nodded *ready*. No further words were needed. From now on the coppers communicated only by sign language.

Going out the door onto the roof, into possible danger, was similar to paratroopers jumping from an airplane. It was the same kind of excitement. Covering each other, the grim little band charged. The morning sun had already warmed the roof.

The policemen reached the blockhouse. Still no resistance, no sign of life. They crept into the short hallway. After quickly clearing the lady's apartment next door, using a key she had provided, they advanced to the second door. Skurzewski's hand snaked around the doorjamb and tried the knob.

The door was locked from inside.

They listened for sounds. They heard nothing.

Skurzewski signaled for the entry to begin. On the count of three. One finger, two, *three*. Gustafson smashed the door twice with his sledgehammer. It splintered and flew open about two feet, stopped by furniture or something wedged against it. Koch behind his shield immediately filled the narrow opening. The shield was black and resembled a knight's shield except for the little window in the middle of it. It exposed nothing of the crouching man behind it except his feet and his gun hand.

"Police! Police!"

Hell erupted. Koch saw Baker, stark naked, roll to one side of his bed as the door crashed in. He grabbed a silver .38 pistol off the lamp stand. Gunfire cracked and crashed in the confined space as Koch behind his shield and the naked man eight feet away dueled it out.

Bullets ricocheted off the shield with the sound of hailstones on a barn. One of them struck with a different sound—the *thud!* of lead smashing bone and flesh. Koch screamed in pain and toppled back behind his shield, blood pumping from his shattered wrist.

Wagner rushed forward to drag the wounded copper out of the line of fire. Connolly took Koch's place in the doorway. There was only enough room for one policeman at a time.

Although everything happened in milliseconds, they seemed like an eternity to Connolly. He hurled his two hundred pounds into a kick that further splintered the door but still failed to enlarge the entranceway. At the same time he snapped shots from his 9mm semiautomatic pistol at the crazy naked man.

Gunsmoke and shadow obscured Baker's form. The room's only light entered in a thin bar through a rip in a drawn shade. Muzzle flashes winked and spat through the dimness.

One bullet shrieked past Connolly's head. Another gouged into the door frame next to his face, spraying splinters into his eyes. He staggered back, all but blinded. With the peripheral vision that remained he glimpsed Gustafson pumping lead from his semiautomatic pistol through the door itself behind which Baker had sought cover.

Connolly emptied the rest of a clip in the direction of the door; his and Gustafson's combined fire riddled it into a sieve. Wood splinters flew.

Strange, frightening thoughts filled the copper's

head. Until now, he wouldn't have thought it possible to think about anything in the middle of a gunfight. Yet, as he received fire and returned it, a thousand images filled his head. It was the first time during his twenty years on the police department that he thought he actually might die.

Judy and Carrie. I'll never see them again. They're at my funeral. All the policemen are there, badges shrouded in mourning black. I'm dead. I can see me dead—

Suddenly, a heavy body fell behind the door.

"The guy's down," Wagner shouted.

The fight was over as quickly as it began. To his surprise, Connolly remained on his feet. Even his vision started to clear. Gun in hand, he followed Gustafson and Wagner into the room filled with the stench of cordite and raw fear and now the heavy metallic odor of fresh blood. Sergeant Ski remained in the hallway working on Mark Koch's wound.

James Baker lay on his back on the floor, bullet holes puncturing the nude pale flesh in at least five places. He was the only occupant; apparently his roommate had cleared out before police arrived. Baker stared at the ceiling while ragged breaths tore through his lips. Connolly knelt next to the dying man; a great sadness overcame him.

"Why did you do it?" he asked.

He had to know.

"James, why did you do it?"

James R. Baker, forty-eight, died without answering. Real life seldom ended like novels and movies. Things did not often come together at the end to make sense.

Afterward, in silence, Sergeant Skurzewski and Connolly helped Mark Koch downstairs to a waiting ambulance. The wounded copper threw his arm around Connolly's neck while the sergeant supported his mangled arm and hand. They went down the stairs together like that—and none of them looked back.

POSTSCRIPT: Officer Mark Koch lost approximately two inches of bone from his right wrist. The five police officers of TAC Unit Five were routinely suspended until the district attorney's office completed its investigation. The investigation was complicated by the fact that all three of Baker's ex-wives joined in a civil lawsuit against the city of Milwaukee and the policemen involved in the shoot-out, charging that Baker had been "executed."

The episode proved especially stressful for the policemen, as it took three months to clear them. Due to the lengthy suspension, friends and fellow officers and even the TAC officers' own wives began having doubts about the shooting. "What did you guys do wrong? You must have done something."

All were finally vindicated, however, when the DA's office issued a new policy that no policeman involved in any future shooting would be left suspended to create public doubt about his judgment. Wisconsin's SWAT association also named TAC Unit Five as its Outstanding SWAT Team of the Year.

About a year following the shoot-out on the roof, Officers Bob Connolly and Richard Wagner chased a car thief on foot down alleys, over fences, and through yards. After the chase, Connolly saw his longtime partner suddenly lurch and fall between two houses. Officer Wagner was dead of a heart attack before Connolly could get to him.

"He was a brother," Connolly said. "He was my brother."

19

Officer Rick Phillips, Tulsa, Oklahoma

September 11, 1991, 3:00 P.M.

For the last ten years of his nineteen-year career in law enforcement, Officer Rick Phillips had lived with his pager. It was as much a part of him as his socks or his underwear. Its beep meant trouble somewhere in the city—a barricaded gunman, some perp threatening to kill his hostage. A job for SOT (Special Operations Team), which is what Tulsa called its SWAT team. Phillips had been one of the unit's snipers for the past three years.

A city psychologist gave him a battery of tests to determine his emotional and mental stability before the sniper assignment. That was followed by a number of graded shoot/no-shoot scenarios. At the conclusion of all this, the psychologist rated him as an individual with a deliberate, methodical, and mature personality. That meant he could shelve his emotions, sight a man through a scope, and drop the hammer on him. It also meant he knew when to shoot and when not to shoot.

During a twenty-six-hour standoff four months ago

in May, the police sniper coolly held his position in an apartment complex on South Rockford while a suspect accused of murdering a former employer and his wife poured more than one hundred rounds of M14 and 9mm fire at police. Several bullets shot off building plaster from the wall next to Phillips, but the officer waited patiently trying to get a piece of the gunman in his scope. He waited hour after hour; his body stiffened and his eyesight blurred from peering through the rifle scope.

The killer was military trained. Not once during the long ordeal did he present himself as a target. He stood back in the shadows away from the windows, released a few rounds, then moved to another window.

SOT finally rigged a Model 1100 shotgun to the bomb control robot. An operator could fire the shotgun using a TV monitor. Space-age stuff.

After an entry team battered down the suspect's door, the deadly little robot scurried inside, prepared to fire, its TV camera searching. The suspect opened up on the machine with his M14 assault rifle, knocking out the robot's TV monitor and blinding it. Perforated like a tin can used for target practice, the robot backed out of the room, clanging and banging like a 1920s Tin Lizzy.

The killer eventually set the apartment complex afire and then committed suicide with a bullet through his temple. Although several people lost their homes and possessions in the fire, no one except the suspect was killed or seriously injured.

That was the nearest Phillips had ever come to killing a man. It was a sobering thought.

As recently as ten years ago, SOT received a callout once a month, if that. It was a sign of the times that in recent years the callouts had become much more frequent—and increasingly violent. Every time the pager went off, Phillips experienced a little surge of adrenaline spurt through his veins.

He experienced that familiar spurt in mid-September when the beeper sounded while he was helping a customer at the police supplies business his wife and he owned and operated on East Admiral. It was near noon; his normal tour of duty began at three that afternoon.

"We have a mental case barricaded in at 7005 East Eighty-ninth Place," Dispatch advised when he called in. "He has access to several guns, has already assaulted officers, and threatens to kill anybody who comes after him. Negotiations have already started."

"I'll be on-scene in less than thirty minutes."

Phillips automatically glanced out the store window to check the weather before hurrying into his private office to change. The sun blazed straight down out of a white-hot sky. He discarded the green OD fatigue blouse because of the heat, donning only a black T-shirt, fatigue pants, and black combat boots. He jerked on his load-bearing vest containing communications equipment, a handgun, and various other pieces of hardware. His rifle—a Steyer-Daimler-Puch .308 with a mounted variable 4-by-12 telescopic sight —lay cased and always ready and available in the trunk of his black-and-white parked outside.

He had never had to use it—but had come close in May with the barricaded homicide suspect.

He sped south through the city streets, on his way to . . .

You never knew how these things might turn out.

An inner perimeter had already been slapped into place to contain the suspect in his residence. SOT leader Lieutenant Burney York gave Phillips and the other men of the assembled teams a thorough briefing at his command post around the corner on Seventy-first Street.

According to him, a twenty-one-year-old diagnosed manic-depressive named Kevin Young had been released from the State Mental Hospital the previous day. This morning he beat his mother with a walking cane and attempted to turn her furniture into kindling. When uniformed patrolmen arrived, he bolted out the back door, hurdling fences and racing across neighbors' lawns. Police pursued him.

Young circled through the neighborhood and returned to his mother's house where he armed himself with a golf club. He charged officers, swinging the club and shrieking, "Motherfuckers! I'll knock your fucking heads off!"

Police reluctant to harm the raging youth retreated to the lawn. Young turned and withdrew into the house, slamming the door and locking it.

"There are guns in there," police were informed. "There are at least two shotguns and two rifles."

That had been over an hour ago.

"Any questions?" Lieutenant York asked.

The teams had been through the drill scores of times in training. Any time an armed man barred himself off against the police, he became dangerous.

Tulsa SOT consisted of three teams of ten men each. Containment teams and entry and rescue teams quickly moved into position while patrolmen on the outer perimeter evacuated the entire block of residents. York deployed his three sniper teams, each consisting of one sniper and an observer. Sniper Team One, Chris Claramunt and his observer, took the southwest corner of the suspect's residence. Kenny Vaughn and his observer covered the rear of the house as Sniper Team Two. Phillips and Joel Spitler, Sniper Team Three, slipped into position at the corner of a neighboring house about one hundred feet southeast and across the residential street from the suspect.

Sniper teams were primarily perimeter protection, guarding the other SOT members during negotiations and any entry or arrest procedures. The same rules of deadly force that governed other policemen also governed snipers. A sniper only fired to defend his own life or the lives of others. Police snipers were not killers. The most successful operations ended with no one getting hurt.

Phillips and Sitler burrowed into a hedge at the corner of their house where, prone, they surveyed the target house. It was a two-story structure with upstairs sliding glass doors on the east side. The doors opened onto a balcony above the garage.

Heavy stone pillars buttressed the front porch. Bushes and a maple in the front yard obstructed a view of the recessed front door. Phillips saw policemen to his left crouching at the corner of the house next door to the suspect's. Two other uniforms—Gho and Walker—hid behind a parked station wagon near the suspect's driveway. Negotiators were on the phone to Young, trying to persuade him to come out peacefully.

It was a wonderful summer's day. Cicada song burred through the heavy air. Phillips made himself comfortable on the ground, settled down to wait developments. At least the ground was warm. He was forty years old. That didn't matter so much in the summer, but lying on ice in a January or February callout left him so stiff after an hour or so that he could hardly stand.

A sniper had to have patience. Phillips had waited six hours at the McCartney Food Stores hostage callout before the foiled robber, an escaped cop killer from Florida, ended it by shooting himself through the heart. It was a twenty-six-hour standoff at the apartment complex on South Rockford before the accused murderer committed suicide.

Who knew how long this one might take?

Phillips scoped the upstairs balcony. It concerned him. Curtains across the glass sliding doors blocked the room beyond from view. A gunman up there on the high ground could pick off targets at will.

"Keep a close watch on it," the sniper cautioned Sitler, who served as a second pair of eyes. Peering through a telescopic sight narrowed your field of view.

Phillips's scope moved on. He scoped curtained windows one by one, what he could see of the closed front door. He scanned slowly. Nothing moved.

He took a deep breath. The first hour after noon began the hottest hours of the Oklahoma summer. Sweat burned the policeman's eyes, trickled in his armpits.

He waited. Waiting was when you thought about the drill, how the target would appear in your scope, his eyes, the trigger squeeze . . .

No different than shooting at a target on the range, you told yourself. But you knew it *was* different. This target breathed and talked and felt. It bled . . .

Phillips waited.

An hour passed before the alert sounded over Sitler's hand radio: *"He's coming out."* Phillips rolled into position. He riveted his rifle scope on the area of the front door, although he could see little of the door itself. Policemen near the house began shouting.

"Put your hands up and come on out!"

The door slammed hard.

"He's back inside!"

A few minutes later, the scene repeated itself, again ending with the slamming of the door.

Back to the standoff. But not for long. The radio suddenly crackled with excitement as policemen at the rear of the house reported the suspect's appearance. He ran into the backyard carrying a long gun, either a rifle or a shotgun. A high wooden privacy fence enclosed the backyard, making observation difficult. Young scurried around inside the fence, occasionally peeping over it as though searching for targets. As he flitted back to the house, he turned at the door and yelled, "You motherfuckers!"

Sitler lying next to Phillips flinched when the gunshot exploded from the back of the house. Muffled by the house between, it sounded like a shotgun or maybe a high-powered rifle. The policemen tensed, relaxing only after Vaughan from his sniper position announced over the radio that no one had been hit.

Young had raised the stakes though.

Phillips swiped his arm across his brow, drawing sweat.

Lieutenant York's voice over the air sounded taut but controlled: *Units be advised the suspect has fired a shot. Green Light,*" he said. "*Green Light. Sniper Team One, did you copy—Green Light?*"

"*Sniper One, 10-4.*"

"*Sniper Two, you copy Green Light?*"

"*10-4.*"

"*Sniper Three?*"

Sitler acknowledged, then twisted his head toward Phillips. Phillips nodded. *Green Light* meant deadly force had been authorized, but it was not an automatic license to kill. It simply warned that efforts to peacefully solve the crisis had failed. It put snipers on notice that the suspect had demonstrated his violent intent and that officers could shoot him if necessary to prevent his harming someone.

Shoot to kill.

Phillips settled himself more firmly against the grass, digging in his elbows. He fitted the leather sling snugly to his forearm and backed the scope off to about a 6X or an 8X to give himself a wider field of view. After all, the suspect's house lay within rock throwing distance.

For nearly four hours negotiators had given Kevin Young every opportunity to surrender. Now, Phillips's hand and eye remained steady as he concentrated totally on accomplishing the task for which he had been trained. That was no longer a man out there; he was a target who threatened the lives of other policemen. If he had to be stopped, and there was no other way, either police sniper Rick Phillips or one of the other marksmen would stop him.

"He's coming out."

Policemen started yelling: "Put down the gun and come on out. *Put it down!"*

Sitler whispered into Phillips's ear, "Do you see him, Rick? Through the bushes?"

"Yeah. I got him."

It was Hemingway who said, *Man is the biggest big game of all.* Something like that. Phillips had hunted big game most of his life. But elk and deer and bear—they couldn't compare to this.

The sniper saw the suspect's gun barrel first. Hedges around the front porch concealed the man himself. The barrel pointed in the direction where Officers Gho and Walker hid behind the station wagon. Sitler murmured something about the two policemen scurrying for better cover behind the nearest house, but Phillips kept his cross hairs trained on the bushes and the gun barrel.

"Give it up. Throw the gun down!" officers shouted, their words strident above the cicada burring.

Minutes passed, dragging.

"He's going back inside," Sitler whispered. Then: "No. No, he's not."

Phillips concentrated on the gun barrel. Slowly, it began moving. He saw the man's left forearm and hand grasping the rifle's forward grip as it appeared past the rock porch pillar. Then the kid himself stepped into view, a skinny youth dressed in black. He crouched, right hand at the trigger of a scope-mounted .270 Sturm-Ruger. Phillips knew his rifles. The kid was as well armed as any of the police snipers.

"He's stalking," Sitler exclaimed, still in his terse whisper.

Every minute detail was clear to Phillips through his scope. He watched as Young advanced off the porch, moving like a still hunter on the trail of a deer. He was obviously dangerous and prepared to fire. His eyes searched, his head ratcheting on his neck, his mouth hard and set. Rifle pointed, he advanced toward where Gho and Walker stood with their backs against the side of the next house.

Phillips had no choice. A policeman was going to die unless . . .

He centered his cross hairs against the left side of the kid's head next to the ear in a nonreflexive area. While a man shot off-center in the brain may flop about like a dying chicken, a man shot precisely through the brain next to the ear dies immediately.

A clean kill. It reduced the chances of the guy jerking the trigger reflexively during his death throes.

Phillips suspended all emotion. He stroked the trigger gently, squeezed it. The rifle recoiled.

The bullet struck Kevin Young like a charge of electricity. Every muscle in his body loosened at the same instant. The .308-caliber slug emptied the youth's brain pan, hurling the bloody contents nearly two feet away from his body. He spun completely around, then dropped to the ground, already dead. He still clutched the rifle in his hands.

Phillips brought the rifle out of recoil, kept it trained on the body until after the SOT arrest team charged forward and signaled all clear. Then, without a word, looking pale and grim, the sniper unloaded his weapon, placed it on the ground, and walked away. The scene now belonged to Homicide and the department's shooting investigations team.

Damn. I would much rather have bought the kid a hamburger.

20

Officer Chuck Foster, San Diego, California

July 18, 1984, 4:00 P.M.

The wonderful California sun reflected July-bright off McDonald's golden arches in the San Diego community of San Ysidro the Wednesday afternoon that James Oliver Huberty, forty-one, burst through the front door of the restaurant dressed in a black T-shirt and military camouflage trousers. Armed with a short 9mm Uzi carbine, a 12-gauge pump shotgun, and a 9mm Browning semiautomatic pistol stuck under his belt, he shouted into the stunned silence that greeted his arrival:

"Freeze! I've killed thousands—and I'll kill thousands more. Everybody get down on the floor!"

Minutes later, the massacre began. The crash and stutter of gunfire, the screaming and wailing of victims drowned out the noise of traffic on busy I-5 behind the restaurant. It became, for statistic-conscious America, the worst single-day slaughter by one man in United States history.

Police officials later reconstructed Huberty's day in

attempting to understand what triggered his bloody assault.

Huberty on that hot summer afternoon would not have been particularly noticed on the streets of any American city had it not been for his armaments. His appearance was well within the boundaries of average —nothing outlandish or bizarre. Short dark haircut thinning with just a touch of gray. Even, well-defined facial features. Not fat, not skinny. Average.

Anyone caring to look more closely might have noticed that he seemed a little harassed, a little drawn. Maybe he had too many bills, employment problems. But lots of people had that look at one time or another.

Anyone looking even closer would not have missed the eyes. The eyes, reflecting the turmoil inside, gave him away. Huberty's eyes had gone mad. On that fateful July day he simply gave up dealing with life.

He had lost his job as a security guard for a nearby condominium complex the week before. His wife remembered his seeming withdrawn and nervous over the loss, but not particularly despondent.

Wednesday began with his appearance in San Diego traffic court for a minor citation. He did not have to pay a fine. Afterward, he and his wife took their daughters, ages nine and eleven, to the San Diego Zoo in Balboa Park. Ironically, Officer Chuck Foster, a SWAT sniper with the San Diego police department, was also at Balboa Park undergoing in-service training. Foster and Huberty may even have seen each other. Later that day they were to encounter each other again in more dramatic circumstances.

The Hubertys were not quarreling, nor had they been drinking or using drugs. The little family appeared normal, even happy, in returning to the rental apartment located about two hundred yards down the street from the San Ysidro McDonald's.

"Everyone is wondering why he would do such a thing," Mrs. Huberty mused later in a letter of apology to San Ysidro. "He has always been a nervous person who could not take much pressure. He had a very unhappy childhood. . . . He came from a broken home. He was always very sad and lonely. His only close friend was his dog, Shep."

A substitute teacher and former welfare worker, she said she and her husband were sitting in their bedroom together after returning from the zoo when he suddenly got up without explanation and changed into a black T-shirt and camouflage trousers. It was about 3:30 P.M., maybe a few minutes later.

"Where are you going, honey?" she asked him.

"I'm going hunting humans," he said.

It was not until later, when she heard the gunshots, the sirens screaming, and then the live newscasts, that she understood what he meant.

There was a crowd at McDonald's. I-5 fed the Mexican border only a mile away, and McDonald's fed the travelers. Most of the diners thought the gunman was a robber.

"Get down on the floor! Get down! Get down!" Huberty raged, jumping about and brandishing a weapon in each hand.

Grandparents and parents and kids—they all abandoned their Big Macs and fries and Chicken McNuggets and dropped bellies-down to the hard tile aisles between the fixed tables and booths. Children whimpered with sudden fright; their frightened mothers attempted to shush them. Let the gunman get what he wanted and leave. No one wanted to attract his attention.

It didn't work out that way. The intruder had a much more sinister purpose. Instead of ripping money from the cash registers and fleeing, Huberty began walking up and down the aisles pumping lead into the prone bodies. He transformed McDonald's into Dante's inferno.

Screaming and rapid gunshots, broken windows shattering, blood splashing, splattering, exploding.

The madman strode around casually pumping lead into heads and faces and backs. Calmly, methodically, like slaughtering penned sheep. Firing alternately from the Uzi and the handgun, reloading one when the other ran out of ammunition. Anyone who moved and attracted his attention, he shot. Some of the people, a few, survived by playing dead. Blood on the floor pooled common underneath alive and dead alike.

Witnesses outside saw a woman hit by gunfire pass her wounded baby out through a broken window into the arms of an onlooker.

"Please take care of her," the woman pleaded before she fell back inside. The onlooker ran with the baby in her arms.

Another woman and her young daughter pulled their car up to the drive-through window.

"I saw glass shattered, things tossed about inside, things not looking normal. So I looked inside and there he was, just shooting. He turned and looked at me, and I put that car in reverse and backed up as fast as I could."

Police Lieutenant Bill Nelson snapped his fingers. "There was a man and a woman walking up to the door, and they were offed—just like that," he said.

Huberty started shooting people outside the restaurant, sniping at them through the broken windows. He shot a driver on I-5. Two young boys rode up on bicycles; Huberty killed both of them.

"They were killed instantly," said Lieutenant Nelson. "They fell facedown against their bicycles, in the parking lot, immersed in blood."

An off-duty McDonald's employee who happened

to drive by the restaurant saw three wounded young-sters outside—one lying faceup, the other facedown, and the third sitting on the grass by the playground had vomited and was bleeding from the face.

"Please help us!" the little boy cried.

"I got out of my pickup truck and started to go toward them. . . . I took off my shirt and tried to put pressure on the side of his face. Then I heard glass breaking and I got down on the ground. By the time I realized what was happening, I just started running. I guess I was lucky I didn't get shot."

The little boy continued to sit on the grass, crying.

Police received the first trouble call at four P.M. and dispatched four patrol units and a supervisor. Radio traffic reflected the confusion as police officers sirened toward the McDonald's on San Ysidro Boulevard, emergency lights flashing.

. . . Report of a 245 shooting, victim a small child, a little girl being taken into the post office across from McDonald's . . .

. . . They've got a description—reportedly the sus-pect is a white male, about forty years old, with a light blue shirt and dark pants. Unknown what his location is now . . . and reportedly it's involved with a rifle, per one witness . . .

712 Nora, I'm taking rounds! We're taking rounds here!

Where are you now, 712 Nora?

I am east of McDonald's . . .

Officer Howard La Bore took cover behind his black-and-white while fire from the restaurant punched holes in his car. He glimpsed the suspect inside walking around shooting out through broken windows. He crawled away from his car on his belly to avoid being spotted by the gunman.

Police quickly established a perimeter to contain the rifleman and evacuate any victims they could reach or who could escape to reach them. At least seven bodies lay strewn about the outside of the restaurant—the man and his wife at the door, the kids on the grass, the two young boys crumpled over their bicycles. Officers soon learned from escaping survivors that the carnage outside was nothing compared to that inside.

Among those who escaped were the manager and his assistant who were working at the back of the store when Huberty entered and began the slaughter. As soon as they saw an opportunity, they bolted out the back door and into the arms of waiting policemen. It was from them that police gleaned much of their intelligence about the gunman.

. . . Reportedly three children have been shot and the suspects are inside the McDonald's. Is it more than one then?

Apparently, from what we understand . . . but we do not know.

. . . Two victims on the north side of McDonald's. Is that in a clear area where paramedics can get to them?

Negative. It's in the line of fire.

. . . We're getting shots fired. We have numerous people inside who are shot. . . .

. . . Repeating for any supervisor to set up traffic posts and lock off the entire area. . . . Get on the air and let's have a traffic post on the south end of Big Bear Center to block off all traffic on San Ysidro Boulevard. . . .

. . . We have a victim of a shooting on the freeway behind. . . .

Okay, several units, we're urgent now. . . . Go ahead regarding your victims. . . .

I have a victim on the freeway with a couple of shots on the leg. . . .

. . . Emergency. I need an ambulance at Smith and San Ysidro—baby shot. . . .

710 Sam. I think you better roll several medevac ambulances. Just have the units with the wounded people advise their locations and we'll try to get them medevac or get somebody to get them out.

SWAT mobilized at four-ten P.M. Some members were on-duty, their tactical gear in their car trunks; others off-duty quickly responded to beepers. SWAT assembled at a hastily established command post two blocks from McDonald's on San Ysidro Boulevard. Scores of curious spectators quickly gathered at police barricades to watch in horror as the action unfolded. Others climbed to the roofs of buildings.

Policemen on the containment perimeter caught glimpses of Huberty inside McDonald's as he continued to spray San Ysidro Boulevard and I-5 with sporadic gunfire. He crouched and ran and peeked outside like a soldier under siege. Officers had strict orders to hold their fire. Witnesses claimed there were at least fifteen people inside with him, maybe more, who might be further harmed by police fire, if they were not dead already.

A blistering hail of semiautomatic fire forced a paramedic unit to retreat as it attempted to reach the downed children in the parking lot. Soon thereafter Huberty shattered the windows of a fire truck. Firemen bailed out and took to their heels with bullets singing after them.

710 Nora—tell the traffic post, don't let the fire trucks in either. We're under, taking fire up there. Let's keep them all out.

. . . 711, can you advise the condition of those two (wounded) that are down at the north side of the McDonald's?

I can't tell. The guy's looking this way. I don't want to move yet.

712 Nora—we have two more . . . inside the post office. One of them has just stopped breathing. . . .

At four-thirty P.M., SWAT deployed dark-clad officers in flak vests to relieve PRT (Primary Response Team) patrolmen on the inner perimeter surrounding McDonald's. An entry and arrest team staged out of sight at the rear of the restaurant. SWAT sniper teams began moving into positions, including sniper Chuck Foster and his observer Barry Bennett. Five hours ago Foster and the madman inside McDonald's had been within hailing distance of each other thirty miles away at Balboa Park. Now, they were on a collision course, as though acting out some destiny ordained by fate.

Foster and Bennett climbed to the roof of the post office just east of the restaurant. Foster lay prone, squinting slightly from the sun. Bennett crawled up beside him with binoculars. From this vantage point they commanded a wide view of the McDonald's and its parking lot, including the playground. Parked cars of customers who were already likely dead filled the lot. The policemen caught occasional glimpses of the gunman scurrying about from one firing position to another. They saw fresh corpses—a leg, an arm, a head. Blood. Lots of blood.

Minutes passed during which an eerie silence reigned. The killer was now finding targets scarce. Police had diverted all traffic within a half mile of the restaurant. Police and medevac helicopters saw the scene from the air as a giant pinball machine sparked by the red, blue, and white light bars of scores of police cars and other emergency vehicles. In the center of the pinball machine sat McDonald's, silent now in the late sun, its windows shattered, bodies sprawled outside. Two or three people still hid behind parked cars, afraid to show themselves in order to escape.

. . . No further on the suspect description other than the fact he's wearing glasses and after he fires one handgun or rifle he reloads and goes to a fresh one. . . .

And does he have camouflage pants?

Affirm. No further on the description. His demeanor is very calm. . . .

. . . Witnesses state there are at least fifteen people still inside and the suspect is listening to the radio.

He has a scanner then?

He's listening to a commercial station.

On top of the post office, sniper Chuck Foster moved to a position farther down the roofline. He peered through the scope of his high-powered Steyer-Mannlicher .308. He had never had to shoot a man with it, had not shot anyone during his five years with the department. But he had trained to shoot men, under circumstances like this.

SWAT Sniper Team One radioed that he and his observer were occupying a ground level window in the post office. Foster, Sniper Two, caught sight of the gunman.

. . . I can see him but I can't take a shot at him. He's behind a truck. He's just standing there walking around. . . .

Sniper Two, which way is he facing?

He's facing the street where the fire truck is parked.

. . . He's behind the counter where the cashier would normally be. Appears he is standing in front of the counter. He's moving toward the front of the building now. . . .

. . . SWAT commander, they don't have a Green Light if he's inside the building with the hostages. . . . If he comes out they have a Green Light. If he's inside with the hostages they have a Red Light. . . .

A volley of fire from the McDonald's chewed up concrete the length of the street in front. *I'm still here,* the volley seemed to signal, *and I'm still dangerous.* It was five-thirteen P.M. The SWAT entry and rescue team waited for orders to charge the restaurant and either slay the killer or take him into custody. Some

165

policemen looked upon such an attempt as certain suicide. Huberty was firing armor-piercing bullets and was obviously a fair marksman.

By this time, police knew their suspect was James Oliver Huberty. His wife had come forward. Huberty was distraught, she said. He was not a Vietnam veteran, as first reports had indicated. Police hated the *Vietnam veteran* tag applied to every madman with a gun. Many policemen were Vietnam veterans.

. . . Advising that the Green Light is on for the snipers. That's the Green Light is on.

Sniper One, confirming. . . . Inside or out?

That's affirm, acting on the information we have here. . . . Inside or out, the Green Light is on for the sniper units. . . .

. . . PRT Leader, can anybody see this guy now?

. . . The guy's sitting down at the front counter. . . .

. . . Team Leader, he's at the counter now. . . . Facing toward the street. . . .

. . . He's probably reloading now. He just blew off another round.

. . . Any second now. . . .

Huberty apparently spotted Sniper One inside the post office. His gunfire spidered post office windows. The police sniper returned two quick shots from his rifle, missing, before he retreated. The long one-sided duel had continued now for one hour and sixteen minutes.

From his vantage point on the post office roof, Chuck Foster caught the suspect in his scope. He saw a pair of legs in camouflage trousers sitting at the order counter. He could not see the man's torso. The man appeared to be reloading the Uzi carbine.

"Okay, I got him. I see him," Foster advised his observer. "I'm waiting for a better position."

One shot. That was what he needed. He waited for the gunman to expose himself more completely. He felt an initial shot of adrenaline, the racing of his heart. He talked himself through it, breathing deeply. Then he concentrated on lining up for the shot.

Huberty slid off the counter and stepped over one of the bodies on the floor as he walked toward the door on the post office side of the building. He stopped about ten feet from the doorway, framed by it. Bodies lay behind him and beside him and in front of him. Foster saw him clearly from the head down. He centered his cross hairs over the gunman's heart.

Their pathways converged. Foster squeezed off a single round.

The rifle recoil went straight back instead of up. The scope remained centered. Foster saw the man jerk and fall back. He thought it curious that his ears weren't ringing from the gunshot. He rechambered a round and kept the scope centered until he was certain Huberty wasn't getting up.

"Keep an eye on him," he told Bennett, who lay looking through binoculars.

Sniper Two, the suspect is down. . . . He's on the floor in front of the counter. It doesn't look like he's moving. . . .

. . . We have had absolutely no movement from inside the McDonald's. Have at least three or four ambulances standing by. We're going to need them.

Sniper Two, I'm watching the suspect. There doesn't appear to be any chest rising at all through my binoculars. He's lying on his back, his head facing west, his hands toward the counter, and his feet toward the street. Like I said, there's been no movement since the shot.

Officer Chuck Foster sat on the roof with the rifle across his knees and waited for the emotional release that always followed a shooting. Afterward, the SWAT executive officer, Lieutenant Bill Becker, offered to take him inside McDonald's, but the sniper shook his head. He didn't want to put his emotions through seeing all the people who were dead.

POSTSCRIPT: The death toll of what became known as the McDonald's Massacre reached twenty-one with the shooting of James Oliver Huberty. Another nineteen were wounded or injured. Huberty's victims included a six-month-old baby, three eleven-year-old boys, a sixty-two-year-old truck driver, and a honeymooner. When he died, Huberty still had a shoulder bag full of ammunition and more out in his car.

21

Police Casualties

The grave voice resonating from New York City's Ninth Precinct station house, eulogizing two patrolmen gunned down in a particularly violent region of the city known as "No-Man's Land," underscored what police officers realized all too well: Bad guys weren't the only ones who died when the lead flew; sometimes the good guys got it too. There are years when as many as 150 policemen die from hostile criminal actions on the streets and highways of America.

Scenes with police honor guards, weeping widows and children, twenty-one gun salutes, and flag-draped caskets with taps playing are reenacted scores of times each year, from New York City to Los Angeles with echoes in small cities and large cities all along the way. The tribute from the Ninth Precinct station house could have applied to martyred cops anywhere in the nation.

". . . The struggle which claimed these two fine young men, the struggle to preserve peace, law, and order at home, is still with us. It is up to all of us, every race and creed, to ensure that respect and honor do not just become a dream or a groundless hope, but a way of life. In memory of Rocco Laurie and Gregory Foster, let us commit ourselves to making this a reality."

Something about the deaths of Foster and Laurie attracted public sympathy; overnight they came to symbolize the thin line of brave men and women who stood between ordinary citizens and faceless predators spreading crime and violence. The President of the United States sent condolences; the Mayor spoke at their funeral. A book was written about them.

Gregory Foster was twenty-one years old, Rocco Laurie twenty-two. Foster was black, short, stocky. Laurie was white, tall, and muscular. Black-and-white. Salt-and-Pepper. Both were ex-Marines who joined the police department and became partners on the Neighborhood Police Team. They were also best friends.

Duty for them on that January 27 began at four P.M. They hit the bricks together, bundled up against the winter in their blue uniform coats. Their beat covered Avenue B from Fourth Street to Fourteenth Street. It was one of the toughest beats in the toughest precinct in the city, the center of drug activity east of "The Demilitarized Zone." Puerto Rican kids called the corner of Eleventh Street and Avenue B *la esquina de los tecatos*—the corner of the junkies.

Citizens on the beat liked the young patrolmen; those who didn't like them—the junkies, the thieves, the dealers—at least respected them as fair and honest cops.

At 10:50 P.M., a control center at police headquarters in downtown New York received a 911 call. When a dispatcher picked up the phone, she heard a woman yelling:

"There's shooting! Somebody's firing shots! . . . They're cops! They're shooting the cops! . . . Oh, my God, they're shooting the cops . . . and they're still shooting. . . . Now, they're running up Eleventh Street. . . ."

When other policemen charged to the scene of the shooting, they found white cop and black cop lying side by side, head to foot. Rocco Laurie was sprawled in the middle of the sidewalk between a bodega and a luncheonette called The Shrimp Boat. He lay on his side, one arm cradling his face. Gregory Foster lay next to him spread-eagled on his stomach, one leg dangling off the curb.

Questioning witnesses, detectives pieced together the details of a planned assassination. The hit wasn't upon Foster and Laurie, the men; it was upon their uniforms. They just happened to be at the wrong place at the wrong time wearing target blue.

At about fifteen minutes to eleven the partners had stopped at The Shrimp Boat to ask about a car parked at the curb. When no one knew anything about it, they continued walking up Avenue B. About twenty feet past The Shrimp Boat, they encountered three young black men walking rapidly toward them. As soon as the men passed, they whipped out pistols and opened fire on the policemen's backs. Detectives later determined that the assailants used three foreign-made handguns—a .38 and two 9mm semiautomatics.

Neither cop had the opportunity to go for his own gun. Foster was hit first. He was hit eight times, three of them in the back. He pitched face forward onto the pavement.

Laurie was shot six times, once in the throat. He staggered on the sidewalk, clutching his throat, before dropping to his knees and then to his side.

"Shoot them in the balls!" a witness heard one of the gunmen shout.

The assailants shot Laurie twice more in the groin as he lay dying. Then they reached down and relieved the policemen of their service revolvers before running toward a getaway car waiting up the street with its engine idling. One of the men paused long enough to tap out a little victory dance in the street, firing his gun wildly into the air.

Two days after the killings, the press received a handwritten letter from the so-called Black Liberation Army claiming credit for the murders. New York police eventually apprehended seven men and a woman for conspiracy to "off" cops.

While it is doubtful Officers Foster and Laurie lived the days of their short careers on the streets under any constant fear that they would be killed, they had to at least face the possibility that it *could* happen. Not only extremists and terrorists stalk the streets itching to strike out at the authority the policeman represents. Common garden variety criminals also go armed and prepared to duel it out with anyone who stands in their escape path. After all, in practical terms the penalty for shooting a cop isn't great enough to deter anyone. Police know that while there may be nonviolent offenses, there is no such thing as a "nonviolent offender."

Officer Irma Lozada found that out when she became New York's first female officer to be killed in the line of duty.

Lozada and her partner were working the LL subway train in Brooklyn when a sneak thief bolted from one of the cars with a necklace in his hands. The partners split up to chase the suspect. That was the last anyone heard from Lozada. Searchers found her body three hours later in the tall weeds of a vacant lot at Chauncey Street and Central Avenue. Her .38 service revolver was missing. She had been shot twice in the head with it.

There is nothing glamorous about dying all alone in a vacant lot full of rubble and garbage. Policemen who meet violent death don't often go out in the blaze of glory. Most cop killings are sadly typical. The cop is simply doing his duty when something unexpected happens.

An FBI study covering the 1980s revealed that of the 947 lawmen slain during that period, most were killed while attempting "routine" arrests. Of the 1,330 individuals identified and charged with the murders, 57 percent were ex-convicts and 41 percent had been previously arrested for crimes of violence. One out of ten had faced prior charges for resisting arrest and assaulting policemen.

The habitual criminal—the common thief, doper, and hustler—is the person most likely to slay a lawman. Vulnerable because of their uniform and public visibility, policemen are not always able to foresee danger or defend themselves against it.

"It's easy to let your guard down," said Detective Austin Roberts of the Tulsa, Oklahoma, police department. "And when you do, that's when you're going to get it. Still, you can do everything right—keep your eyes open, watch their hands, don't trust anybody—and they'll get you anyhow. There are so many nuts out there. Freaks. They can shoot you any time they want and there's nothing you can really do about it."

On an October afternoon, California Highway Patrol Officers John R. Martinez and James Szabo stopped on a stretch of freeway between Los Angeles and San Bernardino to clear spilled debris from the highway. Szabo used his motorcycle to slow traffic and direct it around the obstructed lane while Martinez got off his bike to remove lumber that had fallen from a truck.

Approaching in the westbound lane, an older-model green sedan bulled its way through traffic, swerving and careening and forcing other drivers to give way. Szabo gunned his motorcycle and pulled up along-side the speeding violator. He motioned for the driver to pull over. Two men occupied the vehicle, both "Latino-types" in their thirties.

Instead of pulling over, the driver thrust a pistol out his window. Two gunshots blasted CHP Officer Szabo off his racing bike. Up ahead, Martinez heard the twin reports. He whirled in time to catch two bullets of his own.

Mortally wounded, he crawled to his parked bike and used his radio to summon help: "Mayday. Mayday. I've been shot."

Szabo had been shot in the neck and in the abdomen, Martinez twice in the chest. Szabo recovered, but Martinez died following surgery.

At least a dozen stunned motorists observed the senseless shooting.

"I was just trying to get off the freeway," one excited woman said. "I spotted them after they swerved that big Buick in front of me and almost hit me. I looked inside and saw their faces. They had wild excited looks, happy looks, like the way people look after a football team scores a touchdown. Or someone hits a home run."

The killers turned out to be a pair of wanted armed robbers—Eugene Gonzales, thirty-three, and Thomas Martinez, thirty-five (no relation to the slain officer). Police arrested Martinez in Anaheim, but Gonzales was slain three months later in Salt Lake City during a wild shoot-out that left another lawman dead and one wounded.

"When you walk in and look at the casket," mused a police officer about the death of another policeman, "you know that's ol' so-and-so that got killed. But it could have been any one of you. They shoot at the uniform. You're sorry, but what hits you is, 'It could be me laying there, because I'm wearing the same uniform.' That's what you're really giving a few prayers about. It's not, 'I'm sorry you're laying there.' It's about, 'Whew, that could be me.' Very weird."

Daily, police officers witness human tragedy, degradations, violence. They expect it. They accept it stoically, drawing "shit-proof cloaks" around their emotions to keep what they experience from destroying them. While they are outraged when another cop dies, they are secretly thankful that if it *had* to happen it happened to someone else.

22

Officer Joey Bartlett, Shreveport, Louisiana

July 15, 1989, 4:50 P.M.

Many people when they look at a cop's flashy uniform and the big gun on his hip see glamour, romance, adventure. There he is standing tall, ready to shoot it out with muggers and murderers. That is the image. The reality of the job is quite often something different, something less than the image.

A street cop utilizes much of his time in pursuits much more mundane than chasing bad guys. He is a social worker with a gun—settling family fights, refereeing neighborhood feuds, ticketing motorists, helping elderly sick people back into their beds.

Woman needs assistance. Daughter refuses to take her medication.

Young redheaded patrolman Joey Bartlett snubbed his glasses higher onto his nose and clicked his mike in mild irritation. Another social work call.

It wasn't exactly that Bartlett was disappointed in the job after less than three years on the Shreveport police department. It was just that he was still gung ho. Like most young cops, he preferred chasing cat burglars and hijackers. Action. That was *real* police work. Action. Catching the bad guys.

Bartlett whipped his marked white Ford LTD into a U-turn and resigned himself to answering the call as quickly as possible so he could get back to patrolling. Maybe he'd be lucky tonight and get a burglary in progress. He headed for the Cedar Grove section of the city.

So what was he supposed to do if the bitch refused to take her medication? Send her to bed without her supper? Threaten her? Hold the woman and pour it down her?

It took him a minute, but then he recognized the address. Most of the beat cops did. Dispatch sent him a backup car. The last time police went to Cedar Grove on Susan's medicine, it took four of them to throw her down, truss her hand and foot like a branded calf, and haul her off to the hospital. It would have been easier wrestling down a Louisiana black bear. Some cops said they *preferred* wrestling bears over wrestling Susan.

Susan was a black woman about twenty-eight years old, taller than the average man, and about ten to twelve pounds heavier than a Nissan pickup truck. "That bitch is a beast. She blocks out the sunlight." Every week or so, Susan's mother called the police. Susan was schizophrenic. When she went off her pills, she went off her rocker.

In this business, it seemed, nuts sometimes outnumbered normal people.

Five or six toddlers, all under five years old, played naked in the July afternoon sun, climbing in and out of a junker Oldsmobile abandoned in the front yard of Susan's shack. The shrieking and cursing coming from inside the house seemed to have peeled the paint on the building's outer walls.

Bartlett pulled up to the curb in front at about the same time that his backup arrived. Officer Denise Boddie got out of her patrol car with a nightstick. The sandy blond wasn't very big, but in the macho predominantly male world of the Shreveport police she had built a reputation as a scrapper. Male cops didn't mind answering calls with her.

Bartlett got out with his long flashlight. In some instances it was better than a club.

"Your Honor, I struck the subject in self-defense with my *flashlight,*" sounded less premeditated than, "Your Honor, I whaled the bastard with a three-foot-long club made of hard molded rubber."

"Watch out for Susan," Denise cautioned as the officers walked across the yard, followed by the playing children.

Three or four months before, Boddie's husband, also a cop, answered the Susan call. Susan popped out of a bedroom and shot the policeman with a BB pistol.

From inside the shack came a roar. "You black bitch! You done call the po-lice. I is gone kill you ass!"

Susan had discovered the police officers' presence.

"You ready, Denise?" Bartlett asked with a wry grin.

"Were the Christians ever ready for the lions?"

Bartlett tapped on the door with the end of his flashlight. The household fell abruptly silent. A tall skinny woman let the police officers in. The naked kids trooped in behind.

"It's my daughter again," the woman explained. "I can't do nothin' with that girl. Can y'all carry her to the hospital for me?"

The officers followed the woman down a short hallway to the bedroom at the end, wading through old newspapers, grocery sacks, dirty clothes and soiled diapers, smelly dishes and spoiled food. Cockroaches scurried out of the way.

Susan's bedroom door lay on the floor. It rested on top of all the other litter, which meant she must have recently ripped it off its hinges. The policemen walked across the door into a small dingy bedroom where old blankets and worn-out clothing blocked the sunlight from coming through the windows.

As Bartlett's eyes adjusted to the dimness, they spotted a woman the size of a small cow. She stood ankle-deep in litter with her back pressed against the far wall. Her face and heavy arms were so dark they blended into the pool of shadow created by the black slacks and black pullover she wore. Twin beds narrowed maneuvering room to a short, narrow passageway from the door to Susan.

Susan slashed the fetid air with a long steak knife.

"You muthafucka pigs!" she howled. "I cut you. You come near me, muthafuckas, I gone kill you."

"Go in there, Officers, an' carry her away," Mama suggested.

The police officers hesitated.

If she doesn't want to take her medicine, Bartlett would have liked to say, *then the girl doesn't want it, okay?*

But a cop couldn't do that. Susan was obviously a danger to herself and everyone else. She sliced the air into about a thousand shreds while the officers kept a respectful distance. Boddie began talking in a calm voice, woman-to-woman talk. Bartlett eased into the hallway and used his talkie to request additional assistance. He gathered up the loose children and hustled them to the living room out of the way before returning to the confrontation.

"We're here to help you, Susan," Denise ventured softly. "We're not going to hurt you. All we want to do is take you to the hospital and get you back on your medicine. . . ."

It was like reasoning with a pit bull dog.

"You white honky muthafuckas ain't takin' this fat woman no place, hear?"

Noticing Susan's purse lying at the end of the bed nearest the madwoman, afraid that it might contain a gun, Boddie reached for it with her nightstick.

"Muthafuckas!" Susan lunged forward. She hacked at the policewoman with her knife and grabbed the purse.

Denise fell back to where Bartlett had upended the bedroom door to use as a shield. Susan snatched a long screwdriver from her purse. She advanced on the police officers with the gleeful expression of a maniac, knife in one hand, screwdriver in the other.

Things were going to shit.

Susan kept coming, ignoring the officers' commands to halt. You couldn't just shoot the bitch. It would have been justifiable, perhaps, but cops couldn't go around shooting crazy people.

The officers thrust their door forward to catch the brunt of Susan's charge. The heavy woman collided against it like a Mack truck rear-ending a Mazda. Her knife flicked around the edge of the door, probing for the cops. Bartlett brought his flashlight down on the black wrist with all the force he could muster. Susan screamed with pain as the knife flew across the room.

"Get her!" he yelled, seizing the opportunity.

Using the door as a press, the officers combined their strength to push their assailant back and away. Bartlett grabbed a thick wrist and held on just as Denise lost her footing in the trash on the floor. Everyone went down across one of the beds in a flurry of pumping arms and legs, Denise on the bottom smothered by the weight of the three-hundred-pound behemoth.

In the midst of the cursing and screaming and flying hands and feet, Bartlett held on to Susan's arm. It was greasy with foul sweat. He slapped a handcuff on it, then used the leverage to twist the arm into a chicken wing behind Susan's back. He held on to the loose end of the handcuff; it cut into his hand, but he held on. Handcuffs hanging loose from one wrist were as deadly as a knife. More than one cop bore ratchet-mark scars on his face.

Mama's hysterical voice erupted from the doorway: "Susan, you quit that, hear? Behave yourself."

Susan was in a rage. She was bent on tearing up something. Older cops were always joking that a rookie wasn't a cop until after he butted heads with Susan.

Bartlett saw the gun. All his senses focused on it. It simply appeared in the fight, larger and more real than life, suddenly looming in the gloomy atmosphere. The muzzle six inches away gaped wide in an opening he could have shoved his entire arm down. In that moment, he realized a cop's worst fear—to be shot and killed by his own revolver or the revolver of another policeman.

Susan had somehow torn Denise's .357 from its holster. A .357 ripped a hole through a human being the Budweiser Clydesdales could pull their wagon through.

It was really getting to be a shitty day.

Everything happened in an instant, but it became slow motion for a man pumped up with adrenaline. The revolver spat a wad of flame that, at such close range, appeared like the exhaust from a jet fighter. The explosion in the enclosed room vibrated windows and doors.

Bartlett felt like he had been slugged in the chest with a sledgehammer. The bullet slammed him back against the other bed. He caught himself, gasping for breath, temporarily deafened and disoriented by the discharge.

To describe being shot by a gun to someone who has never experienced it is impossible. No one knows how he will react until it actually happens. Death is, after all, a permanent state of affairs. A man who thinks he is dying often loses concern for everything except his own mortality.

Officer Bartlett panicked. Clutching his chest with both hands, he careened out of the house. *I'm shot. I'm dying. Oh, God.*

The July sun slapped hard against his sweating face, making him realize that he was still on his feet. He paused for breath. Pain contracted his lungs, clawed at his insides. He felt like his ribs were crushed, that his heart and lungs had collapsed.

He keyed his talkie and shouted incoherent phrases into it: "I'm shot! Get me the fire department. Get me an ambulance. Get me *anybody!*"

He looked for blood. There wasn't any. Then he remembered: He always wore his bulletproof vest. But why was he hurting so goddamned badly?

He remembered something else. Denise. She was still in there fighting with a monster nearly three times her size. That thought drove him into action. He turned and lunged back toward the front door, back for that hellhole, just as Big Joe McGrew arrived hot in his cruiser. The cop locked up his wheels and was out of the car and across the front lawn in what appeared to be a single stride.

"Joey, you all right, man?" he yelled.

"I'm hit. Denise is in there."

A second gunshot cracked from inside.

Jesus, the beast had shot Denise.

Expecting the worst, McGrew bowled his way through litter to the deadly little bedroom at the back, gun drawn. Officer Boddie remained very much alive and still in the fight. The two women were locked in mortal combat wedged on the floor between the beds. Denise had latched onto Susan's gun hand like a terrier onto the lip of a mad bull. As Susan fought to turn the gun against the policewoman, it had discharged next to Denise's head, rupturing her eardrum, but the bullet spent itself in a wall baseboard.

McGrew wrenched the contested gun free.

"Susan, what do you think you're doing?" he demanded.

Something about the voice arrested Susan. She stopped fighting. She glanced up from the floor.

"Joe," she said, recognizing the policeman. She lumbered meekly to her feet and stood with her head bowed like a naughty child about to receive a much-deserved scolding.

"Joe, I didn't mean to. I'm sorry," she blubbered.

Denise rose wearily to her feet and watched in astonishment as the woman who had shot one cop and tried to shoot another contritely put her hands together to be handcuffed.

POSTSCRIPT: Officer Joey Bartlett lay on the operating room table at the hospital, prepped for emergency surgery, tubes running into every orifice, before a doctor questioned why a man shot in the chest cavity with a .357 remained conscious and coherent. He checked the wound just below the officer's left nipple. It was ugly and gone to colors. A few drops of blood leaked from it.

But there was no bullet.

When the doctor checked Bartlett's bulletproof vest, a .357 slug dropped out of it onto the floor. He sighed with relief.

"I think you're going to make it," he announced to the policeman, grinning.

When the story hit the press of how a bulletproof

vest saved the life of a city policeman, Shreveport merchants and businessmen took up a collection to buy ballistics vests for every police officer in the parish. Joey Bartlett had bought his own. Paid a half-week's wages for it too.

He has never complained about the investment.

23

Police Chief J. B. Hamby, Catoosa, Oklahoma

September 2, 1978, 8:30 A.M.

At the tag agency in one-horse Catoosa on the Arkansas River navigation channel, Georgia McAfee was on the telephone to her sister, a local school teacher, when two men masked like Old West badmen burst into the office, guns drawn.

Both men appeared in their twenties, one tall and slender and wearing horn-rimmed glasses above his mask, the other shorter and on the heavy side.

"Everybody on the floor!" the taller man shouted.

Before hanging up the phone to comply with the bandits' demand, Georgia whispered a quick plea into the telephone: "Tell J.B. to get over here now. We're being robbed."

The sister didn't have to ask who "J.B." was. It was like a scene out of an old *Gunsmoke* episode: "Tell Matt to get over here . . ." There was no doubt in Georgia McAfee's mind—nor in the mind of any other citizen in Catoosa—but what big J. B. "Red" Hamby could handle anything that came up.

Standing over six feet tall in his boots and weighing

a muscular two hundred pounds, J. B. Hamby, forty-seven, with his Irish-red hair, big white Stetson hat, and ever-present cigar was a man law-abiding citizens loved and lawbreakers feared more than they feared hell. He was widely known not just in northeastern Oklahoma but throughout the state as a no-nonsense lawman tougher than three-strand barbed wire. J.B. "required" respect. He expressed a low regard for anyone who failed to give the law its due.

Fourteen years as a lawman in the Rogers County area had surrounded Hamby with myth. Everyone had two or three stories to tell about his exploits— about the time he cracked the particularly puzzling Verdigris River murder in just twenty-seven hours, or about how in the late 1960s a nationally published hitchhiker's handbook warned "longhairs" and "dopers" to steer clear of Rogers County and J. B. Hamby.

One night, Oklahoma Highway Patrol troopers and deputies in flak vests had an armed fugitive surrounded in a rural mobile home. When Hamby arrived at the scene, officers were crouched behind cars using megaphones in an attempt to talk the gunman into surrendering. Hamby characteristically took in the setting, digesting it slowly as he stood in the open chewing on his fat cigar. Then he casually strolled up to the mobile home and knocked on the door. The surprised occupant peeked out; he was armed with a double-barreled shotgun.

"Look, buddy," Hamby said, leveling his cigar at the man. "I'm going to give you some advice. That gun of yours only has two barrels. It'll take more than two shells to take me. And then you'd better look out."

The startled fugitive meekly laid down his weapon and surrendered.

"J.B. gets rough," said an old woman who had known the policeman most of his life, "but he takes care of us. We don't live in fear of being burglarized or raped in our homes."

An ex-Marine, tough and hard-nosed, the police chief—and only law enforcement officer in Catoosa—firmly believed it was his duty to keep the riffraff out of town and to take care of the townspeople, whatever that required.

After he apprehended a young Catoosa man for a minor burglary, he tossed the kid into the backseat of his patrol car and sped to Tulsa where he screeched to a halt in front of a U.S. Marine recruiting station. He turned in the seat and pointed his cigar at the youthful offender.

"You got a choice," he said. "Go in and join up or go to court and then on down to Big Mac (Oklahoma's State Penitentiary at McAlester)."

The boy got out of the car and went in. Years later, he said, "I'm still scared of J.B., but not the kind of scared you think of when you hear about someone like him. Hell, I'm afraid to do anything bad or he might come and get me. Those years in the Marines were the best thing ever happened to me. J.B. literally saved me from a life of crime."

And so it was that when anyone said, "Get J.B.," everyone knew there was trouble and that J.B. was the man to handle it.

On Friday morning, September 2, at about 8:15 A.M., Hamby was at his usual weekday station in front of the grade school directing children across the street when the robbery alarm sounded on his car radio. A bright summer's sun beamed down on traffic commuting along old Route 66 to jobs in Tulsa. The highway cut past the tag agency located in a small storefront shopping center about a half mile from the old business district of town.

Hamby goosed his big Chevy onto 66, running hot. He jumped the highway median, shot across the opposing lanes of traffic, and whipped into the parking lot of the shopping complex. A two-door blue Pontiac sat by itself on the lot. The chief dismounted, leaving his engine running and his car door flung open.

Inside the office, the two bandits had ordered two women agents and an elderly female customer to lie facedown on the floor behind the counter where their hands were duct taped behind their backs. A Catoosa resident said he saw the big lawman, .357 revolver drawn, charge to the office and jerk open the front door.

"Maybe he should have waited for a backup," Rogers County Deputy Wayne Rice said later, "but that wasn't J.B.'s way of doing things."

The female tag agents thought J.B.'s bold arrival saved their lives.

"I feel like if an officer had come up and said, 'We've got you surrounded,' they would have used us for hostages."

Hamby threw open the door and shouted into the tag agency, "Freeze!"

The stocky masked man turned and yelled back, "All right, you sonofabitch. Don't try to stop us."

Hamby and the two bandits all fired at the same time. Exactly what happened afterward remains unclear. The tag agents and their customer lay facedown behind the counter, unable to see anything except the floor. Outside observers saw only that Hamby bore straight into the gunfight rather than backing out of the office as any other policeman might have done. The door closed behind him.

"As he went inside, there were several more shots fired," said a witness who watched from across the parking lot. "I tried to keep count. I counted ten. I'd hear one, then another . . . then return fire."

Hamby had gone in bigger than life, the way he

lived. Fearless. Standing tall. White hat. Cigar. Gun blazing.

For a few seconds, the shopping center exploded with the sounds of a pitched gun battle. At least fifteen bullets gouged wood, shattered glass, and bit flesh inside the small one-room office.

The taller bandit fired and fell back. His stocky partner in crime snapped off shots, then disappeared behind the counter. Hamby emptied his gun and was apparently attempting to reload when a slug nailed him in the chest, knocking him back against the wall.

The witness outside said Hamby suddenly "came running out" with one of the masked bandits "right behind him." The bandit bolted for the blue Pontiac on the lot while the police chief slowed to a laboring walk and made his way to the Laundromat next door. He was still trying to reload his revolver.

He stumbled into the Laundromat and collapsed to the floor as the masked man alone in the Pontiac escaped on Route 66 toward Tulsa. The second bandit, the stocky one later identified as ex-convict Jackie Rae Young, twenty-nine, lay dead in the tag agency, shot once in the temple and once in the leg. Next to him lay his weapons—a .357 revolver and a .32 semiautomatic.

"Get . . . get some more officers up here," J. B. Hamby murmured to an elderly woman in the Laundromat who came to his aid. She had known the police chief for years. She cradled his head in her arms as he died, shot through the aorta. He had a second wound in the leg.

Hamby had gone out with gun blazing. He died with his empty gun in his fist, still wearing his white Stetson.

"I think he gave up his life for us," Georgia McAfee said. "I really do."

* * *

POSTSCRIPT: About two hours after the shoot-out, Tulsa police arrested another ex-convict, David Gordon Smith, twenty-five, when his girlfriend called an ambulance for him. He suffered from gunshot wounds to the hand and leg.

Bullet fragments collected from Hamby's body matched the .22 caliber pistol Smith fired during the battle. All but one juror at his trial voted for the death penalty. Smith received a life sentence.

In a bizarre miscarriage of justice, the convicted cop killer was soon transferred to a medium-security prison. He worked his way into a program which allowed convicts to go off-grounds during the day to work at civilian jobs. He was allowed weekend passes to go fishing and visit relatives. He bought himself a house and married his girlfriend, all while "confined" to prison.

One day, he went to work at his civilian job and simply did not return. He is still at large.

24

Officer Bernie Swartz, Pinole, California

May 3, 1980, 9:00 A.M.

The mere threat of SWAT often brought gunmen to terms. But Sergeant Mike Weymouth had a different feeling about this one. The slender dark-haired deputy in the khaki uniform was just getting into the defensive driving course he taught at the Contra Costa County Sheriff's Department Police Academy in Concord when the callout came. As commander of the department's nine-man SWAT team, he was ordered to assemble his men at the Pinole police department headquarters. Pinole was a small town of about fifteen thousand, one of a series of communities chained together along the eastern shores of San Francisco Bay by the Pinole Valley Road.

Pinole police had run a wanted woman killer to ground in a thickly wooded area along a creek that emptied into the bay. The fugitive, armed with a semiautomatic Mauser rifle, had already killed one cop that morning.

Weymouth had always been proud of the fact that his men had fired their Heckler & Koch 9mm automatic rifles only once in combat during the ten years of the team's existence. But this time . . .

Speeding as he circled the bay from Concord, he stopped only long enough to pick up his gear from the sheriff's headquarters in Martinez. At the Pinole police department he changed into camouflage fatigues and boots while he waited for other SWAT members. Homicide Detective Peter Janke briefed the SWAT commander.

It started three nights ago, shortly after midnight of April 30, when a woman's screaming awoke residents of Ramona Street. Police arrived to find Rena Aguilar sitting on her porch steps with her belly knifed open and her intestines in her lap. She died before paramedics could reach her.

A witness's description of the van seen leaving the crime scene led to a high-speed car chase starting on the Pinole Valley Road. Officer Larry Dean Hodges chased a green van into the neighboring city of San Pablo, where two men abandoned it on a residential street. Although the officer lost the suspects during the foot chase, detectives led by Peter Janke identified the killer in a follow-up investigation. He was James Richard Odle, thirty-three, an ex-convict on parole who had apparently murdered Aguilar, a friend of his, when she threatened to tell police that he had stolen the van from a car lot.

The investigation brought police to a residence on Alamo Street where acquaintances of Odle said the ex-convict might be hiding. The house appeared empty, although a yellow Plymouth Arrow pickup previously driven by Odle sat parked down the street. Officers staked out the house overnight on May 2. They wanted to be sure he was there before they played their cards.

Pinole Patrolmen Don Donahue and Bernie Swartz

were assigned to the stakeout team at eight A.M. on May 3. After a while, they heard a small dog barking furiously behind the house, sending a clear alarm through the spring morning that something—or someone—was disturbing it. The patrolmen decided Odle may have become wise to them and fled on foot. They checked the house by sneaking up and looking through the windows. Finding it empty of life, they acted on a hunch and followed the sounds of the barking dog.

They advanced cautiously across the suspect's yard, crossed into another yard and climbed a fence to reach Simas Creek. To the south, the shallow creek tumbled out of heavily wooded hills and flowed north to San Francisco Bay between Dolores Court and Hermosa Street.

The policemen separated at the stream. Donahue moved north downstream through heavily overgrown bottom past a liquor store parking lot. Swartz followed the creek bed upstream. The small dog continued barking.

After progressing only a few yards, Donahue found where tall pampas grass had been trampled into a sort of bed. It was like someone had lain there in wait. The rabbits along Simas weren't large enough to make that kind of bed. The officer knelt and looked around, his eyes shifting as they scanned brush and grass for signs of movement.

Although he saw nothing, he couldn't shake the sudden eerie feeling that hostile eyes were watching him.

Cautious, every sense now alert, the policeman followed a trail of bent grass to the creek. He forded Simas using stepping-stones and encountered a well-worn pathway that took him slightly uphill out of thicket to the wide backyard of a house on Dolores

Court. The lawn spread open except for a small olive tree and a ring of tall pampas grass that served as a privacy border.

Eyes darting, Donahue stepped into the open. He had almost reached the olive tree in the middle of the lawn when his restless eyes picked up something in the pampas grass. He froze, squinting.

Then he saw it—the figure of a man hiding in the grass. The man held a sawed-off rifle at port arms across his chest. He was only about twenty feet away.

Yelling a warning to his partner upstream, Donahue dropped to one knee behind the skinny olive tree. He called out to the fugitive.

"You'd better take that weapon by the barrel and toss it out of there, then come out with your hands up. You haven't got a chance. More officers are on the way. The place is completely surrounded."

The man in the pampas was James Odle. He emitted a grunting laugh.

"I sure picked a hell of a place to hide, didn't I? But I'm not going to come out. And I'm not going back to prison."

Police officers are trained to fire only in defense of their own lives or to save the life of another. Although Donahue had his service revolver in hand, held down along his side, he continued to kneel behind the olive tree. It offered scant protection if it came to a fight, but he still hoped to talk Odle into surrendering. At such close range, one or both men would likely be hit if lead started flying. It was an unnerving prospect, but so far Odle made no move to point his weapon.

Speaking soothingly, the policeman pointed out the fugitive's options: "The sheriff's department is sending in its K-9 corps. Listen, man. Throw out that gun and give it up—please? I'd hate to have to kill you. This isn't worth dying over. Believe me, prison is better than dying."

While Donahue continued talking, Officer Bernie Swartz slipped up out of the creek bed, revolver in hand. He burrowed into the pampas grass that also concealed Odle.

"Come on, man," Swartz called out, adding his persuasion to Donahue's. "Just give it up, okay?"

As though surprised by the second voice, Odle rose slightly, prepared to bolt.

"Just stay where you are," Donahue ordered.

Everything happened so unexpectedly that all time before and after seemed to concentrate into the single piercing crack of the fugitive's rifle.

Odle merely shifted the barrel of his rifle and squeezed the trigger. Officer Swartz's knees buckled forward. The rest of his body pitched backward in the grass.

Donahue saw it from his peripheral vision, saw the grass part as Odle burrowed into it like a rat. He released three desperate barking shots from his .38 revolver before throwing caution aside and rushing to his downed partner's side. The only thought that remained in his mind was that Bernie had gone down, wounded, and needed him.

Seeing a partner gunned down is something from which most cops never fully recover. After all, partners spend more waking hours together than they do with their wives. They have shared the ugliness and the danger of working the mean streets of America. They depend upon each other as men depend upon each other in combat.

Swartz bled from the nose and mouth, indicating a probable lung shot.

"He looked like someone had held him upside down and all the blood in his body rushed out his nose and mouth."

Pinole Police Officer Bernie Swartz never regained consciousness. Sergeant Weymouth of SWAT was told

195

Swartz died nearly two hours ago. His killer, James Odle, was still hiding out along the creek with his lethal sawed-off Mauser and, presumedly, plenty of ammunition. Surrounding him was a small army of highway patrol officers, sheriff's deputies, and local policemen. With rifles and shotguns they patrolled Estates Drive to the east and Pinole Valley Road to the west. Others took up sentinel on bridges north and south along Simas Creek.

Detective Peter Janke pointed to a map. "We have him sealed off in this three-block area along the creek," he explained to Sergeant Weymouth. "Some of that brush and stuff is so thick out there that you could step on the bastard before you saw him."

It was like going into a cave after a wounded, man-eating tiger.

"The Green Light is on," Sergeant Weymouth announced to his men. "Shoot him if you have to. Take no further chances with the man."

Before sending his SWAT team into the arena already blooded by the death of one policeman, Weymouth set snipers along likely avenues of escape. He ordered a helicopter from the Park Department to overfly the creek to observe and boom down messages through its loudspeakers.

"Give yourself up," the helicopter thundered from the sky. It whoppered along the creek, rose, and slid into still another approach. *"We have K-9 patrol teams and SWAT teams here now. You have thirty seconds to surrender—or we're coming in."*

Nothing stirred inside the arena of death. This was not going to be as simple as running a scared kid burglar out of a warehouse. Odle had already demonstrated his willingness to kill in order to escape. It would be extremely dangerous going in after the killer—but it had to be done.

Sergeant Weymouth gave the nod to proceed. He looked grim as he assigned four men and two tracking dogs to the first assault element. Too many men in the bush, he knew, and you ran the risk of their mistakenly shooting each other.

SWAT Officer Russ Sutter teamed with K-9 Officer Richard Dussel and his dog to work the left side of the creek. Officer Ken Simpson joined Officer Terry Johnson and his dog to sweep the right bank.

"Take no chances," Weymouth warned them again.

Johnson, carrying a .38 revolver in his hand, worked his dog on a long leash. Simpson remained slightly to the rear, covering with his H&K automatic rifle. Both men wore flak jackets.

They worked their way slowly to the wide backyard where a pool of blood marked the spot of Swartz's slaying. Picking up the killer's spoor, they advanced back toward the creek and its patches of waist-high pampas grass. Both officers suspected Odle had fled the immediate area, either going upstream or down in his desperation.

They walked right into the killer's ambush. The rifle shot from the grass blasted directly into their faces. Johnson went down quickly. He wasn't wounded, but he heard the clap of the bullet as it heated the air past his head and he glimpsed the dark glint of Odle's gun barrel in a patch of pampas grass—a little more than a car length ahead of him.

At point-blank range, Officers Johnson and Simpson exchanged fire with the cornered killer. Lying belly close to the short grass on the lawn, completely exposed, Johnson barked his revolver twice, receiving answering shots from Odle. His dog lunged at the end of the long leash. Simpson from behind the olive tree stroked off two quick rounds.

The second police team, Dussel and Sutter, entered

the fight. Dussel's revolver popped just as a fusillade of bullets chewed up grass and dirt around the K-9 officer on the lawn. Johnson's position was precarious. It was only luck that he hadn't been hit so far.

"Get the hell off the lawn! Get to cover!" Russ Sutter yelled, his H&K cracking on rapid semiautomatic. He emptied a full clip into the fugitive's grassy hide. He slapped in a fresh clip and thumbed the rifle's selector switch to full automatic fire.

"Terry, run for it!" he shouted at Johnson—and emptied another full clip into the grass, the assault rifle stuttering on automatic. The deadly hail of lead ripped through the thick grass like a dull scythe, exploding vegetation.

Bunching his legs, Johnson shot off the ground. He tumbled into the pampas grass along the lawn's border. He was sweating, gasping for breath—but he had miraculously escaped untouched.

So had the fugitive. The officers saw tall grass swaying, then Odle was gone again south up the creek. There was no blood spoor to indicate police may have scored a hit. He remained at large, still dangerous. Still the man-eating tiger waiting in the bush to leap at the throats of his pursuers.

At least seventy shots had crashed along the banks of Simas Creek in the span of a few seconds. The fierce crescendo of fire reminded Weymouth at his nearby command post of a Vietnam firefight. He forced himself to remain with his maps and radios. When word came that his officers were safe, he emitted a sigh of pent-up breath. Map spread across the trunk of a patrol car, the sergeant pondered his options.

His men had been lucky. With Odle choosing the time and place to fight, he could at license pick off policemen all afternoon, then crawl to liberty after nightfall. On Simas Creek, the four unnerved survivors of the shoot-out stood in the bright sunlight.

They looked at each other. Their eyes shifted toward the creek.

They still had a job to do.

Determined that the situation would be resolved one way or another, Sergeant Weymouth settled upon a plan often used by natives in India when they hunted man-eaters. The natives simply spread themselves across the forest shoulder to shoulder and chased the tiger before them into the sights of a marksman. U.S. troops in Vietnam had used the same hammer-and-anvil technique to run an elusive enemy to bay.

Reinforced by a police SWAT team from nearby Richmond, Weymouth formed his heavily armed policemen into a long skirmish line stretching at right angles across the creek. The line would push slowly upstream toward the wooded hills overlooking the bay, either shooting or capturing Odle or driving him into the telescopic sights of a police sniper.

"Shoot him on sight," Weymouth urged. "I don't want any more dead cops."

It was nerve-wracking work. Tension crackled in the air like the snapping of dry twigs beneath the advancing feet of twenty police officers. The skirmish line inched grimly forward through heavy underbrush and thick grass so tall in places that it completely isolated some individuals. Stomachs knotted against the expected bullet fired from hiding. At least you *saw* the tiger when it charged.

K-9 Deputy William Updegraff and his tracking dog ran point for the army, leading the advance. Officer Russ Sutter covered him with an assault rifle. The previous gunfight and its resulting confusion had made Dussel's and Johnson's dogs useless for the remainder of the operation.

Danger sharpened a man's senses, made him aware

of little things he might never have noticed ordinarily
—the snap of a twig, the fall of a leaf, the passage of a
bird. Only adrenaline prevented Russ Sutter from
feeling the fatigue of the past two days as he spear-
headed the mini-invasion with Updegraff. Before the
callout, he had worked a full night shift after attend-
ing a training session the day before. The furious
exchange of gunfire on the lawn, during which he had
emptied two clips, had also taken its toll on his
nerves.

But he dared not relax his guard. The skirmish line
crept slowly forward, all senses as one tuned to the
way ahead.

Events in real life have a way of avoiding the drama
and climaxes associated with TV and novels. Prepared to end the crisis in a final baptism of gunfire, the
police combat line froze when a weary voice called
out from the bushes ahead.

"I'll give up."

Sutter hit the ground. Other officers took cover,
ready for a trick.

"Throw out your weapon and come out with your
hands up," Sutter called back.

"I can't. I've been hit."

"Then hold your arms directly out in front of you
and come on out."

The bushes rustled. A tallish man with long
dark hair emerged blinking into a band of sunlight.
Blood from a minor flesh wound brightened his
left arm. Deputy Updegraff quickly handcuffed the
fugitive.

The word spread quickly: *The suspect is in custody.*
Snipers on perimeter silently slipped their rifles back
into sheaths. Policemen releasing tension through
sudden bursts of talking and laughing gravitated toward the SWAT command post to sneak a look at the

killer who had attracted so much attention. Sergeant Mike Weymouth folded his maps, took a deep breath, then went out to shake the hands of his men coming in with their prisoner.

It was over.

At least until the next time.

25

Officer Robert F. Pyles, Toll Facilities Police, Maryland

September 18, 1986, 8:15 P.M.

U.S. Route 40's Thomas J. Hatem Memorial Bridge, named after a recently deceased politician, spans the Susquehanna River in Maryland to connect Harford and Cecil Counties. At approximately 8:15 P.M. of a rainy September evening, a white step van bound toward the northeast attempted to avoid the toll-booth. It went out of control, careened across two opposing lanes of traffic, and crashed into a concrete median barrier. The driver abandoned it.

A few minutes later, on the opposite end of the bridge, Officer Robert F. Pyles, a patrolman for the Maryland Toll Facilities Police, came upon a young, slightly built black man walking on the bridge. Pyles pulled his car to a stop next to the pedestrian.

"Get in the car," he said. "You're not allowed to walk on the bridge."

Pyles helped the pedestrian into the caged rear seat. As soon as the car started moving again, the passenger apparently decided this wasn't what he wanted. He whipped out a concealed revolver and pointed it through the cage at the officer's head and ordered him to keep driving. For some reason, perhaps because Pyles disobeyed, the gun discharged, splattering the car with blood. The cruiser smashed into a concrete barrier, leaving the officer slumped dying over the wheel and his armed passenger trapped in the backseat and unable to get out.

"Let me out of here!" he yelled when Havre de Grace Patrol Officer Dennis Rittershofer in one cruiser and Deputy Sheriff Stephen Wagner in another came upon the scene. They were on their way to the step van crash. Deputy Wagner had an auxiliary police officer and another civilian in the car with him.

With Pyles draped over the steering wheel, the arriving officers assumed the officer had had a heart attack and lost control of his cruiser. As Wagner unlocked one of the rear doors, the man inside banged it open with his feet and sprang out. In his hand loomed a black revolver.

The revolver barked twice, spitting tongues of flame. The first shot caught Rittershofer in the head, spinning him around and dropping him unconscious to the pavement. The second shot stung Wagner's gun arm. It flapped to his side as he fell back against the car.

The gunman fled on foot into the night, disappearing into the near-deserted streets of Havre de Grace at the end of the bridge.

Soon, flashing lights lit up the bridge—patrol cars, ambulances. Maryland State Police helicopters evacuated the three downed officers.

In the manhunt that followed, police had the advantage of knowing the lay of the 350-year-old town and they had the advantage of numbers. Policemen from adjoining municipalities—Bel Air, Aberdeen, the State Police—as well as officers from the neighboring states of Delaware and Pennsylvania joined to barricade the town and then search it square yard by yard. Residents locked their doors and some of them sat armed with shotguns in their living rooms as uniformed policemen walking and in slow-moving squad cars prowled the streets. K-9 dog patrols sniffed over every yard and vacant lot. Low-flying helicopters played their floodlights into shadows.

"This is the saddest and worst day in all my years of policing," said Havre de Grace Police Chief Earl Walker as he viewed the carnage on the bridge. "In my twenty-five years as chief here, no one has ever been shot."

By this time, police knew the abandoned van had been reported stolen. The suspect was a black male, twenty-seven, Frank Green, a former employee of the van's owner. An ex-convict on fifteen prior felonies, Green had been paroled from Attica Prison seven months previously after serving five years for armed robbery. New York detectives currently wanted him for the brutal rape and attempted murder of a Far Rockaway woman. She had been stabbed five times in the abdomen and her throat slit.

A light rain continued to fall, darkening the night, as the dragnet tightened. Police knew Green was still inside the net. Maryland State Police had contacted the fugitive's father, who told them Green called to say he had shot three policemen and was surrounded by other policemen in Havre de Grace. Phones rang incessantly at police headquarters; frightened residents reported every moving shadow.

Patrolman Charles Briggs III became Green's next victim. He got out of his patrol car to foot search the darkened neighborhood where the killer had last been spotted near a fast-food restaurant. Green appeared out of the night. He bounded silently over a chain link fence and shot Briggs in the back of the head. The officer fell without ever having seen his assailant.

A fast-flying helicopter evacuated Briggs to surgery in Baltimore. Havre de Grace was becoming a combat zone. Four policemen had already fallen to the fugitive's quick gun; officers feared there might be more before the chase ended.

Green lurked everywhere. Sometime during the night he commandeered a moped, but found he could not get past roadblocks. A chain of policemen literally encircled the small town.

As dawn approached, a local handyman made the mistake of going outside to get something from his pickup truck. He unlocked the door before feeling the cold steel of a gun barrel against his temple.

"I'm in trouble," the shirtless man barked. "I want to go to Baltimore. Drive me there."

The handyman drove off in his 1984 Chevrolet pickup with the slightly built gunman next to him.

"Don't stop for anything—or I'll kill you," Green said. "It don't make no difference now how many more I kill."

The truck picked up speed and busted two police roadblocks. Patrolmen gave chase, holding their fire because the truck and driver had apparently been commandeered by the killer.

Suddenly, the frightened driver slammed on his brakes, flinging the killer against the windshield. He bailed out his door as the pickup slid sideways to a stop; Green was out the other door and running, pursued by a hail of police bullets.

The killer disappeared into the dawn, but not for long. Minutes later, a young man and his wife lying in bed with their six-week-old daughter awoke to find Frank Green bending over them pointing a gun.

"I want a shirt and your car," he demanded.

"Hey, man. No problem. Take whatever you want, huh."

Green marched the man outside to a rattletrap 1973 Plymouth Satellite.

"A piece of shit," Green noted, but he took the keys and started it. "You might as well go with me," he said.

"I don't want no part of it."

Green shrugged. He backed the blue Plymouth out of the driveway, tires screeching, and took off. A red streak of dawn wedged itself between the horizon and the black rain clouds of night. It was 6:30 A.M. when the killer rammed through the roadblock at Revolution Street and Juniata. A half-dozen cops opened fire with everything they had.

The Plymouth seemed to explode. Bullets thudded into it, shattering glass. It careened out of control and crashed into a street sign. Again Green survived the gunfire. He fled the wreck, limping a little, dashing into the nearest house by kicking down the door on the run. Bullets splatted into the house around him.

He burst in the front door and straight out the back. A policeman spotted him. The bark of a handgun. Green dropped into autumn leaves. When he attempted to rise again he looked up into an encircling ring of gun muzzles.

"You want to die today, motherfucker?" someone asked.

Green's gun, empty now with every round fired, lay underneath the leaves. More than fifty bullets had been fired at the fugitive during the night; not one had found its mark. When he fell it was because of a leg injury incurred in the car crash.

POSTSCRIPT: Even Frank Green was amazed that he had escaped unscathed. He later confided that Havre de Grace confused him.

"I didn't know where to go," he confessed. "I was running and jumping and hiding. I was even following behind police cars to listen to their radios.

"I stopped a whole lot of times because I was tired. I stayed in a garage, in a truck, and in a car. I almost went to sleep in the car, but something told me to get out.

"I never rode a moped in my life. But I learned fast. I rode it for about two blocks and the police tried to run me over. I started running again.

"I wanted to get up and run (when he was captured), but everybody around me had real big guns. I thought they were going to kill me . . . I think I wanted them to kill me. If I was dead, I wouldn't have these problems. I got to the point where I was so tired of doing everything. I even asked them, 'Why didn't you kill me?' I mean, that would have gotten things over with and we wouldn't have to go to court.

"I'm not trying to be smart, but those pistol experts and marksmen should have hit me. . . ."

Although Frank Green ultimately escaped the death penalty, he was sentenced to four life sentences plus an additional 225 years. According to one estimate, Green would have to be 101-years-old to be eligible for parole. Chances are, however, he will be up for parole long before then.

Officer Robert F. Pyles died in the hospital several days after the shooting. Miraculously, Patrolmen Dennis Rittershofer and Charles Briggs II of the Havre de Grace police department survived their head wounds, although Rittershofer was assigned to civilian duty following his recovery. Deputy Stephen Wagner's arm wound proved superficial; he returned to work shortly after the incident.

26

Officer Scott Rakow, Miami Beach, Florida

June 28, 1988, 4:00 P.M.

Miami Beach undercover narc Efrain Morantes felt a little hinky about the deal. You always felt hinky about a deal this big; hinky kept you sharp, aware; it kept you *alive*. On the seat of the black Ford Bronco next to him lay a briefcase full of reasons to get killed—four kilos of high-grade white Colombian cocaine, four keys of dreams worth one hundred thousand dollars on the streets.

In South Florida, the sun and sea capital of the world, dudes would kill each other for a single gram of coke. Eight police officers in Miami had fallen to gunfire during the last four months alone. Most of the shootings were dope related. Three of the policemen died.

It was enough to make you hinky.

Morantes steered the Bronco onto the Circle K parking lot at the east end of the Seventy-ninth Street Causeway. He parked away from the front of the convenience store. He kept his engine running and glanced at his watch: 3:50 P.M., Wednesday. In the

June afternoon, the narc might have been any Latin man waiting for his wife; he appeared clean-cut but casual in sportswear. Drug dealers these days looked like any other businessmen, except maybe more affluent.

Coke was big business in Florida; it was the state's leading cash product.

A snitch, a confidential informant, had put Morantes into the deal by representing him as a big-time coke dealer. The targets had taken the bait and made an offer for the coke. The only thing remaining on the sting was the exchange. The crime was completed, according to law, once the suspects exchanged cash for drugs.

Morantes was hinky about the exchange especially; you could never fully trust a snitch. Never. Miami police wouldn't even work with this particular snitch anymore.

"He called us this morning," said Miami police Lieutenant Mike Christopher, "and we said no because he has set up a couple of deals in the past that have resulted in police officer shootings. We told him, 'We don't deal with you anymore.'"

Miami Beach police decided to gamble. "He has set up two successful deals in the past," said Beach Sergeant Jim Mazer. "There were arrests made and seizures in both cases."

Morantes sweated freely. The afternoon sun picked pathways of diamonds from the surface of the wide stretch of canal beneath the Seventy-ninth Street Causeway that linked Miami Beach to the city of Miami. No casual eye noticed the stalled Chevy on the corner across and down the street, the leisurely couple strolling into the Circle K for cigarettes, the businessman waiting for a bus.

More than twenty undercovers from SIU (Strategic

Investigations Unit) were stationed around the Circle K to help make the bust once the sting went down.

West of the causeway, at the other end of the bridge, SIU Officer Scott Rakow sat his blue Ford Taurus alongside Seventy-ninth Street, the logical escape route for the suspects if something went wrong. Not that anything would. Rakow yawned, settled into his seat, waited. He expected a more or less routine bust. This time, he was simply holding the horses while the other undercovers got in on the action.

At twenty-eight, Rakow was a four-year veteran of the Miami Beach police department who had gone plainclothes with SIU sixteen months before. Dark haired and athletically handsome, he was a former high school football star who went on to coach at the Hebrew Academy before joining the police force.

He straightened in his seat as Morantes' voice crackled from the police radio. Morantes was wired for sound. "Okay, they're arriving now. That's them in the Blazer."

Two men in a black Chevrolet Blazer eased off Seventy-ninth onto the Circle K parking lot. The driver was a tanned Latin with short black hair and a bushy mustache. He looked to be in his mid-to-late thirties. The passenger appeared much younger—a Spanish type with longish curly black hair and an anxious expression carved into his smooth face.

Cubans.

The Blazer immediately pulled up alongside Morantes' Bronco, driver's side to driver's side. The three men looked at each other before beginning the ritual of exchange. In this business, no one trusted anyone else. It was the most paranoid business in the world.

"Hombre, you have the product?"

"You have the money?"

"Seguro. Of course. Let us proceed behind the building. It is too public here."

Morantes didn't like it. The dope dealers seemed hyper. The driver's fingers drummed nervously on the steering wheel; the other guy, the passenger in the wide-striped polo shirt, his eyes darted constantly.

But Morantes couldn't say no. It might blow the deal.

"Okay."

Undercover cops watched the two black vehicles drift to the secluded gravel near the rear of the Circle K. Plainclothesmen crossed the street toward the store, walking briskly. Morantes got out of his Bronco. The driver of the Blazer got out too, but stood next to his open door.

By the time the narc saw what was going down, it was too late. It was a rip-off, common enough in the trade. One party to a transaction simply decided to take, by force, both the cash and the drugs.

The Latin driver reached inside his vehicle presumedly for his briefcase of money. What he came out with instead was black and stubby and carried with it the sudden impact of opening a drawer and finding a snake. Morantes rushed the man, thinking it his only chance. The MAC-10 submachine gun whistled through the air like a club. It dealt the officer a vicious blow that dropped him to the ground, stunned.

As he struggled to his knees, shaking his head to clear it, action erupted around him. Through a fog he became aware that the Cubans were stealing his Bronco and its cargo of four keys of nose candy.

The older Cuban leaped into the officer's vehicle and stomped the accelerator to the floor. Rear end whipping from side to side, peeling rubber, the Bronco burned off the Circle K parking lot and careened west on Seventy-ninth Street across the short causeway. Engine roaring, gravel flying, the black Blazer followed.

From his stakeout site, Scott Rakow heard the engines, the squealing tires. He saw the speeding vehicles top the gentle rise at the peak of the causeway. Then he heard the stutter of an automatic weapon firing, a sound like the magnified ripping of sailcloth.

As the suspects' vehicles tore off the parking lot, plainclothesmen on foot and in unmarked police cars exploded from every side street, parking lot, and driveway within a block of the Circle K. And the MAC-10 from the Bronco, the weapon of choice among Miami's drug dealers, ripped holes through the afternoon sunlight, the Cuban firing it with one hand out the window while he fought the steering wheel with the other hand. Bullets pocked the street among the pursuing policemen. Stray rounds pierced houses and parked cars, spraying.

Police returned fire.

The driver of a car waiting to make a left turn into the Circle K found himself trapped in the middle of a raging firefight. "It was like a scene out of 'Miami Vice,'" he said. "I started hearing shooting. I tried to duck under my seat, but I'm six-three and it didn't work real good. I looked up and saw two guys—plainclothesmen—leaning on my car with handguns, shooting."

Scott Rakow geared his Ford into the chase directly behind the fleeing vehicles as they passed his point. What began as a "routine bust" had turned into a wild melee. So many police cars—marked and unmarked—erupted onto the causeway, engines gunning, that Seventy-ninth Street became the Daytona 500.

The Daytona with gunfire and sirens.

Police supervisors took over the police band radio, barking instructions. As lead driver in the chase,

Rakow received orders to keep after the suspects, maintain them, but not to attempt to stop them yet. Gunfire still popped from the black vehicles as the suspects attempted to make their getaway. Police cars from Miami Beach and from Miami converged toward the action in a plan to surround the dope dealers and bring them to bay.

It was a short fast chase of about five blocks for Officer Rakow. At the intersection of Seventy-ninth Street with Miami's Bayshore Drive, the commandeered Bronco peeled one direction, the Blazer another. Rakow kept after the Blazer, hard on it. It fishtailed on the curve at Eighty-third Street. Suddenly out of control, it jumped the side easement and crashed head-on into an Australian pine growing in a front yard.

Rakow locked his brakes and whipped the wheel, skidding sideways in the street. By the time he hit the ground running, the Cuban in the striped polo had already abandoned the smoking Blazer. Drawing his semiautomatic pistol, the ex-football player chased the suspect across the front lawn of one house and onto a vacant lot of brilliant white sand and coral covered sparsely with salt grass.

"Halt! Police!" Rakow shouted, reluctant to shoot his man in the back.

The fugitive almost tripped as he turned in midflight to confront the cop. His right hand gripped a 9mm stainless-steel semiautomatic pistol. Rakow brought up his own pistol. Only about thirty feet of bright Florida sunshine separated the two men. Gunshots reverberated through the quiet residential neighborhood.

A teenager working in his backyard near one of the smaller canals that webbed the city heard the gunshots. "I heard four bang, bang, bangs!"

Blood sprayed in a rainbow geyser from Scott

Rakow's forehead. He tumbled like a rabbit nailed in stride. He came to rest facedown, unconscious immediately, his own handgun unfired.

Pursued by other undercovers, the desperate Cuban leaped into the canal in a last effort to swim to freedom. Policemen with pointing handguns lined the canal banks.

"I heard them yell 'Freeze!'" said the teenage witness. "They pulled the guy out of the canal. They were all over him. There were just cops everywhere."

While officers handcuffed a soaked Freddy Andrade, twenty-three, and summoned ambulances for the fallen policeman, other officers chasing the Cuban in the commandeered police Bronco lost him in a residential neighborhood about three blocks away. A neighbor saw the Bronco screech around the corner from Tenth Avenue and swing across the side yard of a bungalow on Eighty-second Terrace. It scooted out of sight to the back of the house, a known hangout for drug dealers.

"It was like a public supermarket over there—cars coming in, out, at all times of the day and night," said one man, who opened his door to see what was going on. Police cars were thick running the residential streets.

A young woman pretending unawareness came out of the bungalow into which the drug dealer fled. "What's going on?" she called out to her neighbor.

"Police are looking for that car that went behind your house," the neighbor shouted back. "I'm calling them and telling."

"No, no!" the woman exclaimed.

She darted back inside.

Moments later, she and a mustached Latin ran out and jumped into a brown 1981 Cadillac parked in the drive. Two blocks away, a patrolman spotted it and flashed it with colored emergency lights. The Cadillac reversed up the street, fishtailing, only to be hemmed in by other police vehicles. Guns bristled around the stopped Cadillac. At the wheel, Felix de la Hoz, thirty-eight, slumped forward in defeat.

"Get out of the car with your hands in sight—or you're a dead man."

Although officers recovered the cocaine from the Cadillac and later seized eleven thousand dollars cash and the MAC-10 submachine gun from the bungalow on Eighty-second Terrace, their loss in the undercover operation proved greater than any gains. Young SIU Officer Scott Rakow lay in the emergency room at Jackson Memorial Hospital with Andrade's 9mm slug lodged at the base of his brain.

For twenty-four hours the comatose policeman fought to remain alive. He died the next afternoon without having regained consciousness. He left behind a wife and a six-month-old daughter.

"It's indicative of the violence in the community, most of which is drug related," said Miami Beach Police Chief Ken Glassman, "and it seems to be unrelenting."

Whenever a policeman dies in the line of duty, his comrades mourn by placing black tape over their badges. Policemen in the Miami area had been wearing black tape almost constantly since February. Two policemen had fallen within the last ten days—and now Scott Rakow.

"When are we ever going to be able to take the black tape off our badges?" lamented Miami Officer Michael McDermott.

27

Cop Humor

Most cops before they become policemen build up a lot of preconceived notions about the job. They have a tendency to idealize it. Going out in the streets to fight crime and evil seems romantic, heroic. Win a few for the Ol' Gipper.

It doesn't take long, however, for stark reality to set in. The job slaughters whatever sacred cows they've been feeding. Coming face-to-face with human evil, seeing the grisly reminders of man's mortality and the broad sweep of his brutality, witnessing crime, insanity, and pointless cruelty—it takes its toll from the policeman's own sense of humanity. Being a cop is to probe into the dark side of American culture; it is a slow descent into cynicism and disgust often expressed through humor. A policeman's humor reveals his dark and macabre view of the world.

Get a bunch of cops together and talk inevitably turns to street whores and junkies, high-speed chases, gunfights and street brawls. Cops' talk is profane, bitter. The things they laugh at—the unusual, the ironic, some grotesque wit of fate that isolates and emphasizes the unpredictability of life—will shock the ordinary citizen.

But what the ordinary citizen fails to realize is that the cops' humor is not simply a reflection of his outlook on society, although it certainly is that too. It is also his attempt to keep at bay the violence and human degradation he encounters daily. It is his way of coping. To laugh at something diminishes its impact, reduces it to digestible portions.

It might appear that policemen are merely calloused and unfeeling, for example, when they laugh and make bets on the exact hour a robbery suspect shot by police will die. While policemen, naturally, *are* hard, tough, what they are really saying through their humor is:

"Look, this shit doesn't affect me. See, I can laugh at it. It doesn't mean a thing. I see it, I'm involved in it, but I just laugh it off and I'm not a part of it, see?

"You take this crap too serious out here and it'll kill you. I mean, people killing each other and robbing each other is heavy stuff. It's bad getting shot at; you can get killed. It's almost as bad having to kill somebody. But if you let it prey on your mind, you'll have a heart attack long before you get your twenty on. Or you'll end up a drunk or in some nut house. The best thing you can do, the *only* thing you can do, is laugh it off.

"If you can't laugh it off, man, you are *doomed.*"

28

Officer Ronald Mallory, Boston, Massachusetts

The copper on the adjoining beat and Officer Ronald Mallory had been parked next to each other talking one slow-action night. Around the corner from them was an auto parts store. The two policemen had just separated to continue patrolling when the beat partner raised Mallory on the radio.

"I hear impact noises around the auto parts," he said. "I'll take the back."

There was a high tin wall, a fence, that ran down the length of the auto parts store. Behind the store was a wide, open field, bisected by a little creek, and beyond that an apartment complex about three hundred yards away.

As Mallory armed with his shotgun sneaked up to the front of the building, he saw the top of a burglar's head through a window.

"Police! Stand up!" he shouted. "Put your hands where I can see them."

The door to the office had been pried open. The burglar walked out with his hands up. But just as he cleared the building, he took off running toward the creek.

"Motherfucker!" Mallory yelled. "He's running south."

Mallory pounded feet down the length of the tin wall after the fleeing burglar. He heard his partner paralleling him on the other side of the fence. The thief struck out across the field, arms and legs pumping. Both policemen reached the end of the fence and dropped side by side to a knee-down firing position.

They emptied their shotguns. They grabbed their pistols and emptied them. Mallory carried two extra shotgun shells in his belt. He flipped one to his partner. They loaded and each fired simultaneously.

The burglar dropped to the ground.

About that time another patrol car rounded the bend across the creek by the apartments. Mallory ran back to his car radio.

"Stop where you are," he radioed the approaching cruiser. "The guy's down in the field straight out from you, about a hundred fifty yards parallel to the creek."

The other policeman walked out in the field and signaled that he had found the suspect on the ground. Mallory and his partner stayed at the auto parts store. They didn't need to go out and see. They figured the guy had to be riddled with bullets.

The sergeant arrived. "Did you all shoot him?" he asked.

The policemen looked at each other. "Was he hit?"

"Did you shoot? Did you fire your weapons?"

It could get sticky. Policemen didn't shoot fleeing felons anymore. Maybe the guy had a weapon himself. Yeah, that was it. They saw what they thought was a gun.

"We're not playing games," the sergeant said. "Did you shoot or not?"

"Yeah," Mallory admitted. "We shot."

"How many times?"

"He shot a couple and I shot a couple."

Later, the shift lieutenant arrived and asked the same questions. "How many times did you guys shoot?"

"Well, I shot some and he shot some."

The lieutenant pointed. "You see that apartment complex? We got damage on twenty-three cars and two apartments."

Holy shit.

"I'm just glad nobody was looking out a window," the lieutenant said.

He was glad.

Rescue came and hauled the suspect. Mallory walked over to the policeman who had found the burglar down in the grass.

"How many times was he shot?" he asked.

The policeman snickered. All the other policemen started snickering. "No, man. He wasn't shot. The motherfucker had a heart attack."

29

Officer Jay Rapp, Miami, Florida

June 16, 1966, 12:45 A.M.

Police partners develop certain characteristics in common which permit them to work together day after day without killing each other. It doesn't make any difference if one of the police partners is a dog; the dog police officer and the human police officer still have to work together.

After seven years on the Miami police department, K-9 Officer Jay Rapp had honed a wry sense of humor to protect himself against the human tragedy he witnessed daily. His dog, Scout, a dark German shepherd weighing over one hundred pounds, had the same kind of humor. The two—man and dog—always seemed to be laughing at private jokes.

Working with a partner like Scout provided assets not *normally* available to other police teams—sharp teeth, a keen nose, four fast feet, and a lawn mower growl guaranteed to ice the blood of any burglar hiding in a warehouse. The term *normally* is used because there have been occasions when regular two-legged policemen demonstrated K-9 dog traits to meet a particular situation.

Take the graveyard shift patrolman who discovered a busted lock on the back door of a hardware store. The shift K-9 teams were busy in the Everglades tracking a pair of armed robbers. Undaunted, the patrolman looked around, shrugged, then shouted into the store: "You got one minute to come out of there with your hands up—or we're turning the dog loose on you."

The cop rattled the back door and emitted a series of growls and eager barks which, had they been authentic, would have come from the throat of an animal the size of a Cape buffalo. Frightened to the paleness of a corpse, the burglar screamed in terror and shot out of hiding. He already had his hands in the "handcuff me" position.

K-9 officers made the patrolman an honorary K-9 police dog and gave him a collar to wear.

Or, take the highway patrol trooper who became known as "Bull Dog" in tribute to his bite. During a throat-grabbing, eye-poking, groin-kneeing scrap with a felony suspect about the size of Man Mountain Dean, the trooper managed to summon help on his portable talkie. After a half-dozen strong cops chained the man mountain to a car bumper, they found one of his ears missing. The trooper had it in his pocket.

"The cocksucker bit me!" Man Mountain shrieked, cradling the side of his bloody head. "The motherfucker done bit off my motherfuckin' ear. Give it back, you fuckin' dog."

"Grrr! Bark!" a policeman replied.

In spite of his great strength and weight, Scout was a gentle dog off-duty. Rapp's baby son rode him around the house like a shetland pony. The dog loved Rapp's wife to the point of adulation. But when he went to work, everything changed. He became a cop.

Police dogs were used mostly for building searches and for tracking suspects. Scout was an excellent tracker, having once sniffed out a lost toddler in a swamp after other dogs failed. Now and again he even nosed out a little dope. But the thing Scout enjoyed most, that set him to grinning and wagging his tail, was being turned loose into a building with a burglar.

During his entire police career he deigned to bite a burglar only one time when he had the opportunity. Considering everything that happened that night, Rapp was reluctant to say the dog's response was inappropriate.

A burglar had hit an electronics appliance store out on Tamiami Trail in southwest Miami. He wasn't the smartest burglar around. Although the crook bore a hole down through the roof trying to avoid the alarm system, he set off an electronic eye once he dropped into the building.

It was past midnight in the middle of the week and things had been dull. Hoping for a little action, every beat cop in the vicinity rolled on the silent alarm call. Four patrol cars, an unmarked task force car, and a vice unit headed in the direction of the break-in, all converging south of the appliance store.

North of the burglary site, Officer Rapp cut off his headlights a block away from the scene to keep from warning the burglar. Scout whined expectantly. They were so bored Rapp had mentioned *hiring* a burglar to stir up a little excitement. Headlights doused, the K-9 officer eased his car into the dark alley that ran behind the row of buildings that contained the appliance store.

The cavalry was doing the same thing at the *other* end of the alley.

Most of the streetlights on Tamiami Trail had been rocked or BB-gunned out, so that the two forces on a collision course could not see each other. Scout panted and grinned in anticipation.

"Keep quiet, Scout. You'll get your chance, ol' man."

Suddenly, flashlight beams at the other end of the alley lasered the night, flicking about like dueling "Star Wars" sabers. Rapp and Scout heard shouting as from a mob. "Halt! Police!" And a lot of other things like, "Motherfuck! Stop, you sonofabitch!"

And: "Halt, or we'll shoot!"

Holy Christ!

The burglar flushing out the back door of the electronics store ran for his life. Rapp glimpsed him silhouetted against the police flashlight beams. Pursued by the thundering hooves of the police mob and their shouted warnings of "We'll shoot! We'll shoot!" the burglar fled down the alley directly toward the unseen K-9 car.

The most dangerous place in the world was downrange of a bunch of excited cops.

Rapp fumbled for his headlights switch. But it was too late. The crackle of gunfire sounded like a sprung ambush in Vietnam. Muzzle flashes resembled furious fireflies.

Rapp rolled into the floorboard and tried to make himself as small as a field mouse. He felt he could have hidden underneath a leaf, underneath a pebble. He wanted to crawl into the air vent.

Scout in his backseat cage was smart enough to belly onto the floor himself as window glass shattered and started flying. The radiator went with a hiss of steam. Bullets clanged into the car with the impact of heavy hail on a tin roof.

Rapp's yelling and screaming and the dog's barking turned off the crescendo of fire like someone had flipped a switch. Cops came running up. Flashlight beams probed the mangled vehicle.

"Oh, my God. We've kilt them."

Rapp stirred.

"No. He's *alive.*"

The officer slowly rose from the floorboard, brushing broken glass from his uniform and checking himself for bullet holes. Scout from the backseat cage informed everyone in no uncertain terms what he thought of things. Rapp climbed out of the car, still amazed that neither he nor his dog had been hit. He looked around at the circle of policemen.

"You damned fools," he snapped. "Now, where's the burglar?"

The cops shuffled uneasily, glanced at each other.

"I guess we missed him."

Shaking his head in disgust, Rapp brushed the rest of the glass off his uniform and, without another word, let Scout out of the car. They still had a job to do. Rapp led the dog down the alley until they crossed the burglar's scent. The cowed policemen followed in a little knot of embarrassment.

"Seek," Rapp encouraged his dog. "Scout, seek."

Scout's upper lip quivered in disapproval of what the onlooking policemen had put him through, but his love of the chase and of the reward at the end—biting the burglar—quickly overcame his ire. Rapp unleashed him. Nose down on the scent, the big shepherd followed it in a straight line from the alley to a place where weeds and bushes grew next to a fenceline.

That was where the thief hid. He lay belly down on the ground with his arms and hands wrapped around his head. Although unscratched, faring better than the K-9 car, he was scared to within a heartbeat of dying from fright.

Rapp saw Scout sniffing at something. It couldn't be

the burglar; Scout would have already had a bite of him. Scout sniffed again, and, then, at about the same time that the approaching policemen recognized the trembling mass of flesh on the ground . . .

It was the most eloquent testimony possible under the circumstances. It was better than words, better than biting. Scout notified everyone, including the thief, of the humiliation he had suffered from all concerned.

He hiked his leg—and thoroughly soaked the cowering burglar with his contempt and disgust.

30

Officer Chuck Sasser, Tulsa, Oklahoma

October 13, 1971, 5:00 P.M.

Sasser learned about the house from an informant, a snitch whom he busted for possession of a stolen auto tape deck. That was one way you created a snitch— bust him, then deal out the charges for a better bust.

"I can help you, Officer Sasser," the slime ball whined, pleading like a cur caught in a chicken pen. "Don't put me in jail. I know things."

"Who'd tell a fuckface like you anything?"

"I'll find out things. Man, I'll work for you."

Sasser held the tape deck over his head like a hammer. "Produce," he advised, "or I go to the DA."

The house was the first solid intelligence the snitch had turned in in over a month. He called and Sasser met him in a sleazy Dawson bar. The officer wore jeans and a loose lumberjack shirt to hide the big .357 magnum thrust into his belt. He was a member of the plainclothes Tactical Squad, a dirty dozen assortment of specially selected cops assigned to chase felons and slam their asses behind bars, no matter what it took.

"You know Bonnie Kansas?" the snitch asked,

whispering out the side of his mouth like Sidney Greenstreet on the *Movie Classics* channel.

The Kansas clan was third generation scum. Bonnie's granddad ran moonshine when Oklahoma was dry. Her daddy was a pimp and a bookie. A year ago her elder brother threatened to shoot the tonsils out of the next cop who attempted to arrest him.

Sasser grinned, remembering the warrant that came out charging Clyde Kansas with auto theft. Clyde hung around his scummy bars, posturing and embellishing his crime exploits for the next crop of admiring and envious young punks who might not yet have been to that criminals' finishing school, the state pen.

"Tulsa cops are cowards," Clyde said. A rough-looking man in his thirties. Scars enough to play a TV bad guy. "They know I'm wanted, but they don't have the balls to arrest me. They know I'll kill 'em if they try."

Sasser tracked Clyde to a north Tulsa pub. As usual, the ex-convict sat at the bar holding court. The guy had a reputation to maintain. The plainclothesman attracted little attention as he sauntered across the crowded tavern and approached Kansas from behind. The guy was on overdrive, his lips flapping like a loose sail in a storm.

Close to the fugitive, Sasser rammed his index finger hard into the man's back, then stuck his head around to the side so Kansas could see who it was. The cop grinned into a face gone suddenly pale.

"Well, Big Mouth," Sasser drawled. "Here's your chance. Either put up and kill me—or walk out of here while you're still alive. You're under arrest."

He dug his finger harder into the ex-con's back. Sullen tension filled the barroom. Everyone fell silent, waiting for mean Clyde to live up to his boasting.

"Well, Mouth?"

Big, tough Clyde Kansas got sullenly off his bar stool. There were a few preliminary sniggers when the patrons saw it was a *finger,* not a gun, that was marching Clyde out the door. Then the entire barroom full of drunks and dopers and thieves and lowlifes burst into raucous laughter. That was one bar to which Clyde Kansas would never return.

Yeah. Sasser knew the Kansas bunch.

"Clyde Kansas is out of prison again," the snitch said.

Nine months in the pen for auto theft and burglary. Sixth conviction. That was about right. Sooner or later, the Department of Corrections would rehabilitate Clyde if it kept trying.

"Bonnie owns a vacant house on the east side," the informant continued. "Clyde and a couple of other dudes are doing a bunch of residential burglaries. They fill up Bonnie's garage with stuff, then about once a month they back a U-Haul up to the door and take the goods to St. Louis where a fence takes it off their hands.

"They're all ex-cons. They got guns and they're always packing. I know they'll use them if they're cornered. Now, is that good enough to get me off the hook?"

Sasser managed to get a look inside the house to verify the information. It was a frame cracker box studded onto a sleepy side street in east Tulsa. The attached garage was full of TVs, stereos, furs, jewelry, guns, small appliances. Enough hot items for spontaneous combustion.

It wasn't enough to *know* thieves were ripping off the city. A cop had to prove it legally beyond a reasonable doubt. What was reasonable to the average man wasn't always reasonable to lawyers and the court system. Sasser wanted to catch the thieves with the goods. It was hard for a lawyer to dispute reasonableness when you caught a bunch of ex-convicts gloating over a garageful of hot TVs.

The policeman found a friendly neighbor down the block and parked his unmarked car in the drive. He sat there for a week with binoculars, waiting for the burglars to return. His vigil finally paid off.

A gray Chevy sedan occupied by two hardcases eased down the street late one afternoon and pulled to the curb in front of Bonnie Kansas's house. It sat there for a few minutes, engine idling, while the two men ratcheted their necks, looking around for cops. Watching through binoculars, Sasser recognized one of the men as Pete Diggers, Clyde Kansas's former cellmate. He felt disappointed that the other man wasn't Clyde, but what the hell. You took what you were handed.

After a while, apparently satisfied that all was clear, Diggers turned the Chevrolet into the garage drive. The two men got out of the car and went inside.

A few minutes later they started loading their car trunk with items from the garage. Good enough. Sasser decided to bring them down. He radioed for a backup as the ex-cons finished their business and backed out of the drive. He fell in behind them in his unmarked.

Most habitual criminals can spot a cop faster than a hooker can pounce on a twenty dollar bill. Almost immediately the guys turned hinky. Sasser saw Diggers glancing into his rearview mirror. The passenger shot a quick look back over his shoulder. The Chevy whipped a right and cut through residential streets.

They had to be stopped—now. Before they had a chance to get into traffic and run. Sasser flipped on his side cherry. To his surprise the Chevy pulled immediately to the curb. The men sat in it, unmoving, bent slightly forward. Their mannerisms—the way they stared directly ahead, their hunched-forward posture

—caused the cop to smell a rat. And a good thing he did. He learned later that each thief had a loaded revolver held down between his legs. They were just waiting for an opportunity to knock off a nosy cop and make their escape.

Sasser came out of his car with a 12-gauge shotgun. Using the open door as a shield, he leveled the cannon on the heads of the two men.

"Police! Get out of the car. Slowly."

Neither man moved. They still contemplated a shoot-out, debated it in their minds.

"Pete, you know goddamned well I mean it," Sasser said. "I'm giving you ten seconds."

He racked his shotgun. Nothing sounded more like bad business than the well-oiled mechanical *ker-chunk!* of a round of double-00 sliding home.

"One . . . two . . ."

Diggers jumped out of the car in such a hurry the nails in the soles of his shoes kicked sparks off the pavement. He knew the proper drill; he had been through it often enough. Trembling from adrenaline flow, he automatically spread-eagled himself over the hood of his car.

"I'm out of it," he screamed. "I don't want no part."

The passenger kept his seat. Sasser lodged the bead of his shotgun barrel against the back of the guy's head. If the thief so much as breathed deeply, his brain would be all over the nearest sidewalk.

"Three . . . Four . . ."

"I'm giving up!"

The burglar's door opened slowly. He crawled out with a sheepish look and meekly assumed the position. His head hung low between his outstretched arms. A slight breeze wafting down the street brought the cop a disgusting odor. He was twenty feet away from his prisoners, but he still gagged.

"Jesus H. Christ!"

The guy had pumped so much adrenaline trying to work up enough guts to come out of the car with gun blazing that he lost control of his bodily functions. It was damn tough to have a decent shoot-out with the cops after you had just loaded your pants.

Nothing is worse than the stench of fear filling a man's undershorts.

Backup arrived, engine blowing. TAC Officer Craig Roberts jumped out with his revolver drawn.

"Take that one, Craig," Sasser said quickly, pointing. "I'll take the other one."

Roberts started forward, then stopped like he had run into an invisible wall. He caught his breath. "Goddamn, this sonofabitch has shit his pants. I'm not transporting him in *my* car."

Sasser grinned. He already had Diggers handcuffed. "Hey, I have mine; you have yours."

Roberts drove his prisoner to the police station with his head stuck out the window of his car. The humiliated would-be gunfighter sat silently handcuffed with his chin resting on his chest. His arrival at the station house cleared cops off the first floor from the booking desk to the officers' lounge.

31

Police Combat Fatigue

The names policemen invent for sections of their cities reveal their awareness of the city as battlefield: "Combat Alley," "Little Vietnam," "The War Zone," "Bloody One Precinct," "Fort Apache." Even if an officer never fires his weapon in anger, he still perceives his environment as hostile and threatening. The next trouble call, the next moment, could erupt in violence. While it may not be war in a classical sense, it is nonetheless *war*. More important, the policeman sees it as war.

Conventional soldiers know who their enemy is, even when fighting a guerrilla war such as Vietnam. The enemy either wears a uniform or has assumed characteristics which mark him as overtly hostile. The enemy is recognized as an enemy, is considered an enemy, and the soldier fights him as an enemy.

The policeman in his war enjoys no such luxury. His enemy is never clearly defined. He blends with the population and becomes a foe only when he chooses to commit a crime. The cop knows he has enemies, but never specifically who they are or when they will choose to strike. Maybe he is the next traffic violator, at the next family disturbance, around the corner at the convenience store, in tonight's dark alley.

Combat soldiers endure relatively short periods of intense action, followed by "stand down." They look forward to when their ordeal will end and they can return to the "real" world. The cop's world, on the other hand, *is* the "real" world. His adjustment to combat is permanent. Policemen sustain lower but more steady levels of tension over much longer periods of time.

Policemen and combat soldiers adapt to war's absurdities, mutilations, evil, degradations, and suffering in similar ways. They learn to dull their senses to avoid emotional blowout, to accept violence on a level which permits them to function mechanically without their emotional machinery breaking down. It is the only way they can survive.

"What is happening to you?" a policeman's wife demanded in horror after he shot a criminal in a gunfight. "Have you become so hard and calloused that you can kill another human being and it doesn't even bother you?"

The policeman knew something had happened to him, but he didn't understand what. He knew only that whatever it was affected the way he interacted with his wife, children, parents, and friends.

"It is left up to cops to do the dirty work," he explained. "This shit has to rub off on you. I recall being at a party with some of my wife's friends and I was telling an incredibly funny story about how this flasher sat in a park with a hat over his lap. Every time a woman passed by, he lifted the hat to expose himself. My partner and I were working vice. We waited in the bushes—and as soon as a girl walked by and he exposed himself I shot his dick with a BB gun.

"Well, I looked around and nobody was laughing. Cops would have been roaring, because they identified with the situation. But here these people, including my wife, were scandalized. Five years later my wife divorced me. She said I wasn't the same man she married. I wasn't."

The police world is a macho world. A cop is always tough, strong, in control. Anything less is looked upon as a weakness. A cop takes great strides to hide his feelings, even going so far as to deny he has them. Fellow policemen shun the officer who lets a tear fall at the scene of an accident fatality, who fails to laugh at the prospect of an armed robber getting a bullet of his own. Officers suspected of having emotional problems are reassigned to the "rubber gun squad," a stigma that follows them for the rest of their careers.

In recent years, psychologists have taken a closer look at the policeman and his reaction to his job and environment. They discovered that police officers suffered from "combat fatigue" the same as combat soldiers. In fact, they may be even more vulnerable to it than soldiers are. A shocking number of policemen felt varying degrees of isolation and alienation from society.

When alienation was directed inwardly, "combat fatigue" exhibited itself through fits of depression and lingering anxieties. The victim had difficulty forming strong emotional ties. He internalized, suppressed. He sometimes described himself as feeling numb, as though nothing could ever touch him emotionally. Policemen suffering from the condition had notoriously high rates of divorce, alcoholism, and suicide.

Typically, a homicide detective battled depression and insecurity for years, unable to escape the stark reality of the streets to maintain a normal life. Living itself seemed pointless. His wife divorced him. He quit police work and began shifting from job to job. At last account, he was gambling heavily, drinking to excess, and was on his third divorce.

Another typical example was the patrolman who got off-shift and then sat in his car at the station house parking garage and shot himself. Cops call it "eating your gun." The victim left poignant testimony to the results of police combat fatigue.

"I just couldn't take it any longer," he wrote in his suicide note.

Police expressions of rage and frustration directed outwardly sometimes become socially unacceptable, such as the incident in Los Angeles where a group of officers beat a motorist. In other incidents, a cop shoved two burglars off the roof of a building when they refused to climb handcuffed down a ladder; two policemen caught a child molestor and threatened him by hanging him upside down off an expressway cloverleaf; vice cops cornered a known dope dealer, thief, and pimp and cut his ear off to mark him.

"Actually, we didn't cut it off. We only notched it a little."

During street rioting in Miami, a veteran policeman endured two days of random assault, arson, and looting before something snapped. Rioters hurling everything from rocks to old auto carburetors had him pinned down with several other officers in a dark alley. Suddenly, he sprang to his feet and rushed into the open with his revolver drawn. Like a man gone mad, he emptied his weapon shooting into the tenements that surrounded him. He reloaded and, more deliberately this time, fired six more rounds.

Afterward, he strolled alone down the alley—and not a single brick came his way.

Police brass rushed him to the hospital. His condition was never diagnosed as "police combat fatigue," but that was exactly what it was.

While most cops manage not to commit police

brutality, eat their guns, or become alcoholics, few escape completely the complex effects of police combat fatigue. Until fairly recently when police departments started hiring psychologists, officers suffering from job-related stress had nowhere to turn for legitimate help. People outside police work would not understand. The policeman himself often did not understand—and even if he did he went to extremes to deny it.

In his classic book, *The Onion Field,* ex–Los Angeles cop Joseph Wambaugh relates the tragic story of a cop killing and its aftermath. The most poignant theme of the book is how watching his partner get killed affected Officer Karl Hettinger.

The murder case dragged through the court system for ten years. Guilt-ridden and plagued by nightmares, suffering from severe psychological trauma, Hettinger lost weight and actually shrank in size. He was frequently impotent and depressed and gradually withdrew from social contacts. Eventually, the police department fired him for shoplifting.

When the officer's attorneys finally won him a disability pension from the Los Angeles police department, he became one of the first examples in police history through which psychiatrists officially recognized that policemen are psychologically damaged by trauma associated with police work, especially when violence is involved. A police officer did not have to be shot to become a casualty; there were other ways he could be victimized.

"I do not know of the arrangements which the police department has for psychological assistance," doctors wrote during their assessment of Karl Hettinger, "but I urge that very careful consideration be given for the *prevention* of mental and emotional disturbances arising from traumata in the line of duty."

Trauma-associated disturbances later applied to returning Vietnam veterans would become known as *Post Traumatic Stress Syndrome*. It was a condition cops waging war in the streets of America had suffered all along. Unlike soldiers who eventually escape to return to "normalcy," the policeman never signs an armistace. His war—and the casualties that accompany it—will never end.

32

Lieutenant Bill Butler, Miami, Oklahoma

May 20, 1992, midnight

Domestic disputes. Family fights.

"I'd rather be thrown into a pit full of starving lions than into a house where the husband and wife are feuding," decided Lieutenant Bill Butler of the small-town Miami, Oklahoma, police department. "The lions are more predictable."

After fifteen years in uniform, Butler still carried a solid 185 pounds on his five-ten frame. He looked younger than his forty-one years until you saw the eyes. The eyes were the sadder, wiser, older eyes of veteran cops who have seen it all.

Who have seen it all.

On a cool spring night in late May, the lieutenant assumed command of the graveyard shift and was knocking off a few minutes' paperwork when he heard the dispatcher assign a fight call to an older residential section on "O" Street N.W. Family fight, the dispatcher said.

Ordinarily, Butler would have noted the call and monitored it routinely. He had three policemen patrolling the city of fifteen thousand on the midnight shift—Sergeant Jeff Coble and two patrolmen, Brad McMinn and Kelly Witten, all capable of handling a domestic. Only, the lieutenant recognized the address and knew instinctively that it meant trouble.

The Swiggerts lived at that address. Raymond Swiggert was one of those tattooed two-hundred-pound "good ol' boys" who hung around bars picking fights with smaller, meeker men. Still under thirty, with a drinking problem that turned an ugly-tempered man uglier, he delighted in boasting around town that the Miami cops were afraid of him. He had already served one term in Big Mac, the state pen, for cattle rustling.

A braggart, a bad egg, a drunk, a wife beater. Such was Swiggert's reputation. His wife had earlier filed for a protective order against him claiming she was in fear of her life. Apparently, Swiggert was back, violating that order.

As the sergeant and the two field officers whipped their cruisers northwest, speeding through the nearly deserted streets of Miami, home of Northeastern Oklahoma State College, Lieutenant Butler turned over the engine of his own cruiser and headed their way.

Just in case.

Later, the policemen learned that Swiggert and his wife had reconciled and gone out on the town together. The wife's fourteen-year-old daughter and seven-year-old son from a previous marriage were watching television when the couple returned home. Swiggert staggered through the front door and cast a bleary look at his stepdaughter.

"You're drunk again," the girl said with long-suffering disgust.

"Who the fuck you calling drunk?" Swiggert retorted.

The teenager got up to retreat to her bedroom. Swiggert started after her. His wife intervened. Sometimes it took very little to release the rage that always seemed to simmer in the big man's boiler. With practiced efficiency at such things, Swiggert ripped the door off his stepdaughter's bedroom and threw it into the hallway. He roughed up the girl, throwing her around, slugged his wife a few times for good measure, and finally threatened a neighbor who heard the rampage and tried to stop it.

Police were roaring down the street to the rescue when Swiggert ran out of the house and jumped into his black Mustang. He peeled backward out of the driveway so recklessly that his stepson, who was dashing for help, missed death or injury from a rear fender by mere inches.

The Mustang took off up the darkened street with tires squalling, pursued by Sergeant Coble and his two patrolmen in separate cars. Drunk and still consumed by rage, Swiggert led the cruisers in a wide fast circle through the neighborhood. He cut corners, spun out and careened off curbs, gunned his engine furiously and screamed profanities out the window.

Officer McMinn anticipated the fleeing man's route. He whipped his patrol car onto a side street, cut ahead of the speeding Mustang, and slid his car sideways to block off the end of the street on which Swiggert lived. The cruiser's emergency lights lit up like Christmas as the Mustang exploded onto the other end of the block.

Swiggert locked all four wheels. Gears scraped. The Mustang reversed, fishtailing. Patrol cars bore down on him from behind. Trapped, Swiggert whipped the black vehicle to the curb in front of his own house. Policemen saw his large figure sprinting for the door. Inside the house, the drunk grabbed his blond wife and stepdaughter and dragged them by their arms to the back bedroom.

Police crashing through the door after him heard him shouting and raving like a lunatic. Guns drawn, they pushed their way down a short cluttered hallway, stepping over the ripped-off door, and in the bedroom came face-to-face with every policeman's worst nightmare.

Swiggert perched on the edge of his bed, his eyes rolling whites, while with one big foot he pinned his stepdaughter to the floor. He had his wife in a neck lock across his lap. The wild spray of the woman's long hair hid her husband's hand held at her throat. Her eyes flashed round, startled, like the eyes of a deer caught in headlights. Unmoving, she appeared as stiff as a clothing store mannikin.

"I'll cut the bitch's throat!" Swiggert roared. "I have a knife. I'll kill the slut. I swear I will. Stay back, you fucking pigs, or she's dead right in my lap in front of you."

Raving. Like that.

The little girl was sobbing on the floor.

"He really will kill me!" the wife cried in abandoned terror. "If he says he'll do it, he'll do it."

"I'll cut the bitch's throat!"

"He'll do it. *He'll do it!*"

"I'm enroute to the scene," Lieutenant Butler radioed. "Advise officers on the scene to hold everything just like it is. Let's try to get it calmed down."

Patrol cars with emergency lights flashing tri-colored studded the lawn like it was a giant pinball machine. Two or three off-duty patrolmen kept curious neighbors at bay. As Butler pulled up and dismounted, he heard Swiggert ranting from inside the house. He heard the wife's voice high-pitched with fear and pleading. He heard the little girl crying.

Jesus, what a way to start a shift.

He took a deep breath and proceeded briskly across the porch and through the front door. The house closed dirty and unkempt around him. Typically low-class. Dim lights glowed; the TV was still playing. Butler focused on McMinn, whom he saw through an open door at the end of a short hallway. McMinn was pleading with the unseen suspect, one hand reaching placatingly while the other hand gripped his service revolver.

Deeper inside the room stood Witten, also with a gun in hand. Sergeant Coble held ground just outside the doorway.

The voices babbled together.

"Look, fella, let's not do anything foolish. We can talk about it, okay?"

"He's got a knife!"

"Mama! Mama! Oh, please let her go!"

"Let's just everybody calm down," McMinn continued, his voice easy and low and controlled.

"Fuck you!" Swiggert shouted. "I'll cut the bitch's fucking throat. I'm ready to die right here with her."

Butler later learned that one of Swiggert's relatives in Missouri committed suicide by pointing a loaded gun at a policeman and forcing the policeman to shoot.

"Shoot me!" Swiggert now screamed. "Kill me—'cause I'm gonna cut her throat."

"He really will kill me," shrieked the terrified wife.

Fucked up.

Butler slipped his .38-caliber service revolver from its holster. He held it out of sight alongside the seam of his trousers as he eased into the room. Swiggert remained focused on McMinn and McMinn's gun. The revolver, Butler noted, was cocked.

McMinn cast a quick glance at the arriving shift supervisor, then fell gratefully silent, deferring the situation to the lieutenant. Butler filled in smoothly. He began talking, calmly, soothingly. The soft words tumbled out:

Let's end this thing right now before somebody gets hurt. Tell me your name, come on, fella, let's talk, tell me your name and let's talk about it 'cause nothing's worth all this and you don't want to hurt your wife you know you don't and I know you don't and look at your little girl how we're all scaring her and none of this makes sense and if we can talk about it . . .

Like that.

The blond wife's eyes closed and her lips moved rapidly in silent prayer. When her eyes opened again with startling impact, she whimpered, "Oh, he'll kill me. He'll kill me. He said he would and he will. He's got a knife."

Butler saw into the man's eyes. He saw nothing rational in them. The guy listened to nothing except his own inner rage.

Listen to me mister please listen to me and don't hurt the lady and give me the knife and let's all calm down and talk . . .

The light in the room was low-wattage. Shadows crept up walls and into cheeks and into the hollows below eyes. Tension so filled the room that Butler felt hair all over his body crackling.

"I'm going to cut her throat. I'm going to do her," Swiggert said matter-of-factly.

He twisted slightly on the bed, bringing his wife around. With abrupt horror, Butler realized that the man had lost all ability to reason. He thrust his wife forward so police could watch the blood spurt from her jugular when he slit her throat.

"I'm going to do her!"

In the streets a cop faced with a decision like this had maybe an instant to make up his mind and act. Later, the courts argued at their leisure for months, even years, about whether or not he made the right decision.

I can't let him kill her and do nothing!

Butler dropped to one knee to gain a more advantageous angle of fire. At the same time, in the same smooth motion, he brought up his .38. He aimed it at the contorted face partially obstructed by the woman's. The sight blade lodged against Swiggert's forehead.

No time to think.

Just to act.

Butler squeezed the trigger.

The clapping bark of the discharge, the resulting muzzle flame and smoke, set off the home fire alarm system. A small red hole appeared magically in the direct center of Raymond Swiggert's forehead. The house alarm screamed as the policeman's bullet slammed the crazed man against the sheets. He died instantly.

POSTSCRIPT: Afterward, shaken and pale, Lieutenant Butler waited outside until Police Chief Bill Melton arrived to initiate the shooting investigation.

"What kind of knife was it?" Butler asked.

"Bill, there wasn't a knife. He didn't have a knife."

"What!"

"Bill, listen. You couldn't have known. You did what you thought you had to do."

It was hard enough squeezing a fatal bullet into the forehead of another human being. For Lieutenant Bill Butler, it was even harder having to tell his wife and sons, his mother, his friends that he had shot and killed an unarmed man.

"I'll agonize over it the rest of my life. I'll always see that face and wonder if maybe there wasn't something else I could have done. You know you did what you had to do, but still you wonder. . . ."

33

Officer Dwight Stalls II, Newport News, Virginia

July 16, 1989, 4:00 P.M.

It was the same goddamned nightmare every night. Like he was dying. Like he kept dying. Sweat streamed from his body, soaked his bedclothing. *Blink! Blink!* went the orange camera flashbulbs as a gun with a muzzle the size of a water pipe pumped lead screaming and tearing into his body. Explosions crashed through his brain, mangling it; it threatened to burst from his skull.

Every night the doper came and killed Officer Dwight Stalls all over again. The guy stood in the doorway with his big gun and maniacal laughter exaggerated and made hideous by monsters of the policeman's own subconscious. Stalls kept trying to shoot the guy back. But it was like in dreams where the snakes were chasing you and you were falling off a cliff and you couldn't move to do anything about it.

Stalls bolted upright in bed, gasping for breath like his lungs had bullet holes in them.

Everything was okay in the bright reality of daylight —but nights he died a little. It showed in the grim and unrelenting set of the young officer's face. Only a sheet of crisscrossed nylon a quarter-inch thick—his bullet-proof vest—saved him. Sometimes he took out the vest and thrust his finger into the bullet hole.

"Statistically, it'll never happen to you again," the shrink assured him.

Stalls had been too young for Vietnam, but the department psychologist said he suffered from stress symptoms like those of a combat veteran.

"Most policemen retire after their twenty without ever even firing their gun at a person," the shrink said. "I'd say it'll never happen to you again."

Two years had passed since the shooting in the raid on the dopers' pad. It wasn't only the shooting that bothered him, Stalls admitted; it was the fact that the police department still had not officially recognized the action. Other cops were decorated for things like helping little old ladies across the street. What had he received for getting shot in the line of duty?

The returning Vietnam vets had not received their parade; neither had Stalls. He thought he knew why.

Shortly after the shooting he got into a row with a female police officer. What with equal opportunity and the feminist movement, politically correct speech and all that, it was the kiss of death to even suggest, for example, that a lady cop five-feet-three inches tall and weighing one hundred pounds was not at least a police*man's* equal in a bar fight with two-hundred-pound stevedores. Although the shooting and the policewoman had nothing to do with each other, Stalls felt the department had withheld his medal to punish him.

It was a fucked up world.

Police work had lost much of its attraction. After the gunfight, the department transferred Stalls out of vice and back into uniformed patrol working the day watch. Writing up burglary reports from overnight break-ins, issuing parking tickets. It was an older cop's dream to "retire" to day shift with weekends off. Although Stalls wasn't an older cop—he had nine years on the department—he carried such bitterness around with him that all he wanted to do anymore was answer his radio calls and be waiting at the station house when it was time to go off watch.

He hated a late call. That was the reason he uttered a short curse that July afternoon when the police dispatcher assigned him a disturbance at a trailer court on Jefferson Avenue. *". . . Several drunk and disorderly discharging firearms . . . No backup available . . ."*

Stalls rode a single-man unit. Normally an officer never went alone to a gun call. Glancing at his watch—it was quitting time, Bud time—he snatched his radio mike.

"10-4. I'll advise on backup when I arrive."

Most disturbances were bullshit anyhow.

He tramped the gas pedal and sped north on busy Jefferson, one of the main thoroughfares through Newport News. A group of people in front of Arch's Trailer Court saw the patrol car coming through traffic. They ran out waving their arms and yelling. Stalls stopped thinking *Routine* and changed it to *Maybe we got a problem here.*

The trailer court, a known trouble spot, stretched back from the street for more than a block. It was a jumble of cheap and junky trailers occupied by lower-income whites—drunks, unemployed laborers, welfare mamas. They were always going off on each other.

The patrolman whipped his car onto the graveled horseshoe entrance. Everybody was trying to talk at once. Stalls heard "shots" and "they're shooting back there."

"Just calm down," he said. "Where is all this happening?"

A kid of about eighteen offered to act as guide. Stalls radioed in his situation, then followed the kid along narrow trailer court streets littered with abandoned junk cars and old bicycles. The other residents stayed behind to huddle around a phone booth, as though for protection.

The policeman's guide directed him down one street, then across to another, cutting between trailers.

"They're right around the corner," the kid whispered, hesitating.

Most of the time police arrived after a disturbance was over. Stalls hadn't heard anything so far—no gunshots, no quarreling. But he did notice that parents had all their children off the streets.

Let's get this over with and go home.

It was so unexpected—the clap of the single gunshot reverberating through the flimsy trailers—that it startled the kid; he seemed to leap twenty feet into the air. Stalls crouched instinctively into a defensive position and slapped for the holstered 9mm semiautomatic that the department had started issuing to replace standard service revolvers. He recognized the gunshot as the cracking *boom!* of a high-powered hunting rifle.

Somebody meant business.

Weapon in hand, the blue-uniformed officer darted around the end of one trailer and emerged onto another street. The kid followed. The first thing that caught Stalls's attention was the figure of a tall skinny man standing in a trailer doorway less than seventy feet away. The man gazed intently in the direction of the phone booth at the distant entrance to the trailer court. He appeared to be testing the still summer air before he levered another round into his .30-.30-

249

caliber hunting rifle. He hadn't seen the policeman. He slowly raised the rifle as he prepared to fire again.

The gunman's appearance burned itself into Stalls's memory banks, as such things will when the body goes into the fight-or-flight mode. The low sun highlighted the red in the man's unkempt beard, it sheened off sweaty bare arms extending like muscular sinews from a dirty T-shirt. He appeared to be in his late thirties, maybe older. The bill of a ball cap shaded his eyes.

At the time Stalls had no way of knowing what was going on. Later, he learned that the man with the rifle and another man inside the trailer were feuding with their neighbors across and down the street. For the past fifteen minutes the guy had been steadily pumping lead into his enemy's trailer, round after methodical round, while his enemy hugged the floor and prayed for either divine or police intervention.

"Police officer!" Stalls shouted in his best authoritarian voice. His knees were bent into a combat position, his pistol aimed. "Drop the gun!"

What happened next was like out of one of Stalls's worst nightmares. The bearded man turned toward the policeman's voice in one smooth motion and pointed his rifle. Maybe statistics were against it happening again, but it *was* happening. For the second time in less than two years, Stalls stared horrified down the muzzle of a gun barrel.

Thoughts roared through the officer's brain at warp speeds. He experienced old familiar dark emotions all at once—fear, dread, hatred, sadness. Like when the doper shot him, and he shot the doper back.

Jesus Christ God, not again!

Not *again*.

The bearded man pulled the trigger. The angry crack of the bullet superheated the air near the policeman's head.

It wasn't a nightmare. This was *real*. It was real and

Stalls wasn't paralyzed as in the nightmares. He reacted out of training, smoothly, professionally.

The piercing *bang!* of his pistol merged with the echoes of the deeper-throated rifle. The impact of the 9mm bullet knocked the rifleman sprawling back through his trailer door. From a distance of sixty-nine feet, Stalls's combat marksmanship nailed the man one-half inch above the left nipple. He died instantly.

A second man appeared in the door and wrenched the rifle from his downed comrade. He sprang onto the small porch deck and leveled the weapon at Stalls as Stalls streaked for the cover of a nearby tree. Stalls fired his 9mm twice more and was astonished to hear the barking of another pistol to his left and rear.

Officer Barry Haddix had broken all speed records in his haste to reach an endangered beat partner. He was too late for the first rifleman, but his pistol now cracked twice. The second gunman crumpled to the deck of the little porch, where he lay moaning slightly and twitching, all the fight taken out of him. Although two of the four police bullets found their mark, the guy lived to face trial.

It was all over in a matter of seconds. The kid—Stalls's guide—had watched it all, having dropped to the ground as soon as the bearded man turned his rifle against the cop.

Stalls smelled the acrid odor of gunsmoke. He felt the late warm sun on his face. Sirens began to wail in the distance. He stepped slowly out from behind the tree and gripped his pistol so firmly his knuckles turned white. It kept his hand from trembling. His gaze fastened upon the two bodies—one already a corpse—in the door of the trailer.

He dreaded the night when the nightmares returned.

34

Detective George Haralson, Tulsa, Oklahoma

November 8, 1982

Detective Sergeant George Haralson was a natural character actor. It made him Tulsa's best vice cop and the nation's leading authority on child pornography. It also made him a good police hostage negotiator. Whenever necessary, he suspended all emotion, all personal feelings, and immersed himself into playing whatever role a situation required.

One November night, the police character actor met the cop killer. Six hours later, Haralson had the killer convinced that his only friend in life, his only salvation, was a police officer. Trouble was that sometime during those hours—Haralson didn't remember exactly when—he stopped playacting. He *became* his role. He got caught up in the strangest and most demanding emotional struggle of his life.

Around 9:30 P.M. that Thursday night, Haralson and another vice cop busted the clerk of an east Tulsa adult bookstore for peddling kiddie porn. While they were transporting their collar downtown, a distinctly different drama started to unfold at McCartney's Supermarket on Tulsa's south side.

A lone gunman brandishing a .38-caliber blue steel revolver invaded the supermarket. Wired as tight as the magneto on an antique Ford, he tossed a couple of cracking shots into the ceiling to get everyone's attention. Customers at the checkout lines screamed and cowered against each other.

"This is a robbery," the bandit announced.

Cowboy boots made him almost six feet tall. The gun added another three or four feet to his stature. He was no doped-out kid either. The man appeared to be in his forties. Hard, rough; that narrow, mean ex-convict look.

"Don't worry about paying for your groceries," the robber snapped at the customers. "Just get 'em and get out of here."

Loaves and cartons and boxes flew all over the floor. People rushed, screaming, to the doors.

"They didn't have to pay for them groceries or nothing, but they just dropped them and ran. Can you imagine *that?*" the gunman mused later, as if wondering how people could have been so foolish to blow the opportunity to get something for free.

After ordering clerks to fill a paper bag with cash from their station registers, he grabbed it and thrust his gun hard into the store manager's back.

"You and me are gonna take a little walk out to your car," he said. "Everybody else just stay put—or he gets it. Understand?"

The two men strode into the night. The other employees watched, frozen to their stations, as the bandit escorted his hostage across the wide parking lot. There were only a few cars parked about. The men had almost reached the manager's car when another car pulled into the lot off South Memorial. Its headlights washed across the wide sheet of pavement, momentarily distracting the robber.

The manager seized the opportunity. He flung his car keys against the asphalt and bolted. The bandit snapped two shots at the frightened man's back, missing both times. Then, apparently mistaking the approaching car for a police cruiser, he wheeled and lunged back into the supermarket.

Frantic now with fear of his own, shouting and threatening, he corraled six employees—an older woman named Lois, in her forties; a stock clerk in his early twenties; and four teenage girls, one of whom could not stop screaming—and herded them into the manager's office. By the time he realized that the arriving car wasn't a patrol car, it was too late. Black-and-whites, real ones, were converging on the building like hounds, surrounding it and trapping the gunman inside with his hostages.

"I'll kill 'em. I'll kill 'em!" he screamed.

Downtown booking his prisoner into jail, Haralson received the summons for a hostage negotiator. He was one of only five trained negotiators on the department. He shoved his collar at his partner—"Here, book this guy for me!"—and took off in his unmarked low rider.

McCartney's looked like a police substation, there were so many black-and-whites and unmarked detective vehicles on the lot. Dark-clad men of the Special Operations Team, SOT, which is what Tulsa called its SWAT, had already staked themselves out with rifles among the canned goods.

The trapped bandit and his six hostages occupied a small walled-in office near the front of the store at the far end of the row of checkout counters. The office was slightly elevated to provide an overall view of the store's interior from a single small window. It had only one door, closed. Haralson heard a girl wailing in the office. A man cursed her, then yelled a warning at police: "Don't try to come in here on me. I swear I'll kill 'em."

Departmental policy assigned to the case the first negotiator to arrive. Patrol Lieutenant Bill "Tank" Thompson directed Haralson to an interstore telephone at one of the checkout counters that was protected from the gunman's view. The stocky plainclothesman took a deep breath as he reached for the receiver and slipped into his role. On his patience and skill rested the lives of six people trapped inside an eight-by-ten-foot room with a man who had already demonstrated his contempt for life by firing shots at the escaping store manager.

Haralson started to sweat.

Police hostage negotiators were especially trained to handle desperate people while maintaining an even, conciliatory temperament. They were prepared to haggle for hours. The longer the negotiations continued, the greater the disadvantage to the hostage taker and the more likely the incident would end without violence. Demands from the suspect were met with small concessions from police, but only after reciprocal concessions from the hostage taker. The idea was to swamp, overwhelm, and confuse an offender with details, stalling the process, while at the same time making him think the negotiator was doing everything within his power to satisfy his demands.

It was a dangerous tightrope to walk. The object was to eventually wear down the hostage taker to the point where he simply gave up. *If we give you this, you have to give us that. But it'll take time to get what you want. We'll have to work out a lot of details.*

Haralson picked up the telephone, dialed. He heard the phone ringing in the office. The gunman picked it up immediately.

"My name's George Haralson. We're going to see if you and I can't work things out here."

"What? What did you say? I can't hardly hear you. This bitch in here is screaming and carrying on too much. She's hysterical."

"Kick her out then," Haralson replied quickly. "I can't hear you either. Kick her ass out of there so we can talk."

"Just a minute."

The office door opened. A screaming teenager flailing her arms fled down an aisle until a SOT officer grabbed her and rushed her out of the building.

It had been almost too easy.

"What's going on in there?" Haralson asked.

"I just shoved her out the door. It's a lot quieter in here now."

Negotiations began. Soon, the policeman and the robber worked around to first names. It was "George" and "Joe." Haralson learned that the man was Joseph Raymond Greer, forty-two, who had escaped from a Florida prison detail. He had been serving a life sentence in Raiford State Penitentiary for murdering a Hollywood, Florida, police officer. His main beef, now that he had been trapped and forced to come up with one, was that the Florida Department of Corrections and the Justice System had treated him unfairly. He had been convicted of three felonies prior to his slaying the policeman.

"Everywhere I go," he complained, "if there's a crime committed they blame it on me."

Greer didn't know what he wanted to do about it, other than for the police to go away and let him leave.

"Joe, let's just keep working on this and see what we can come up with."

An hour passed.

"Joe, ordinarily I couldn't offer you anything 'cause I don't have the money to pay for it. But, hey, we have a whole store here. What do you want—something to drink, cigarettes, doughnuts? I mean, hell . . .''

"All right. How about a Pepsi, George?"

"Great. Now, we got a little problem here. How are we going to get it to you?"

Haralson negotiated the delivery of the Pepsi into another half hour and the release of a second hostage. As soon as one of the remaining teenage girls came hurrying to freedom, Haralson himself delivered the Pepsi to Greer.

Greer opened the door cautiously, his revolver trained on the plainclothesman. Haralson made quick mental notes on the man—longish dark hair permed around a face lined-out with tension, a muscular man wearing a black and silver pullover shirt. The dark eyes in the pale face appeared haunted, trapped like an animal in a cave.

"Glad to meet you, Joe," Haralson chirped. "How's it going?"

"Likewise good to meet you, George. But I've had better days."

They both laughed.

Four hostages remained in the office with Greer as the wrangling continued and midnight dragged weary heels through the supermarket. SOT snipers waited patiently. The fugitive proved too careful to expose himself for a clean killing shot through the window. Besides, because of the possibility of a hostage getting caught in crossfire, the SOT commander kept the Red Light *on*.

"I think I can get him to come out of there. Give me time," Haralson requested, sweating.

Almost three hours passed. The two men continued their chatting over the telephone. They talked about the football strike, their childhoods, their families, rapping like two old friends. Sometimes they hung up the phones for a few minutes, giving Haralson a much-needed respite. He felt drained, drawn between his job and a growing sympathy for the desperate plight of the convict trapped as much by his own past as by the police.

Sometime after midnight, Greer traded still another teenager for a long-distance call to Florida to speak to his mother.

"You don't need that many people in there to mess with anyhow," Haralson assured him. "One will do just as well as three or four or six."

"George, I trust you," Greer said.

"I trust you too, Joe. I know you don't want to hurt anybody else."

"I don't, but I will if I have to."

With three hostages left, Greer decided that what he wanted to do was go live on TV and explain how he had been mistreated.

"That sounds reasonable to me," Haralson replied, "but it'll take a little time to work it out. Just hold on and I'll start things going."

Cameramen from all three major Tulsa TV stations were in the parking lot filming live what they could of the unfolding drama. Although any of them would have risked life and equipment to do an on-camera with the gunman, Haralson dragged Greer's demand into another two hours.

"George, these women in here have to take a piss," Greer complained.

"Let them come on out then," Haralson suggested.

"I can't do that."

The negotiator took a trash can to the office to be used as a potty. A short time later, Greer complained, "George, it really stinks in here."

"There's a simple solution to that, Joe. Let the boy carry the trash can out."

"It does really stink. It's making me sick."

The stock clerk carried the trash can out. That left two hostages.

For hours Haralson and Greer had focused on each other in a situation fraught with such tension that they might have been the only two men left on earth. The man in the office, Haralson discovered, was a real human being just like everyone else, no matter what he had done. Psychologists have pinned a name to a phenomenon that occurs when people taken hostage begin to identify and empathize with their captors. They call it the Stockholm Syndrome.

Haralson was as much a captive to Greer over the telephone as the two women in the office. He understood how the older captive, Lois, felt as she progressed to calling Greer "Joe" and urging Haralson to concede to his demands. He could kill her at any time, on a whim, but she was no longer afraid.

Stockholm Syndrome.

"George," Greer telephoned, sounding agitated. "I asked for that TV camera more than an hour ago."

Haralson edged his voice just enough to show that he was trying and felt put-upon.

"Joe, you think you got problems. I got you in there, I got the SWAT team wanting to go after you, I got the brass on my ass, and I got these TV stations arguing about whose camera to use. I'm doing the best I can. Give me a break."

Greer giggled. Tension dissipated. "See what you can do, George," he said.

"It's like this, Joe," Haralson continued conversationally. "We all have our problems. I was having problems once and a friend bet me that if I took all mine and put them on a table with everybody else's, I'd probably take one look at all their problems and pick mine back up and put them in my pocket."

Greer laughed—and traded his remaining teenager

for a TV set so he could see himself when he finally went on the air. That left Lois in the room. By this time Lois didn't want to leave Joe alone at the mercy of the police.

"George, I feel like you're my best friend, my only friend," Greer said.

Haralson glanced up from the telephone toward the office. Heavily armed police officers occupied strategic positions throughout the store. Haralson had to remind himself that the gunman was a cold-blooded killer, a man still dangerous. He had to keep reminding himself of that.

It was decided that Haralson would take a TV camera into the office to film Greer rather than risk providing the fugitive with another hostage. Shortly before three A.M., TV cameramen loaded the cop with camera, battery packs, and other equipment. Feeling like an overladen pack mule, Haralson checked the handgun thrust into the belt of his trousers along his spine and staggered down the narrow passageway to the office. Greer let him in.

For the next twenty minutes, the two men conducted one of the oddest performances ever filmed for a TV news station. Sweating heavily from exertion as well as fatigue and tension, his tired brain wrapped in cobwebs, the policeman struggled to keep in focus as Greer, who stood stiffly in front of the camera, revolver pointing, rambled bitterly on about what society had done to him.

Greer explained how he was a three-time loser who had "accidentally" shot a policeman during a jewelry store holdup. He hadn't done nearly all the things he was accused of doing, he said, and he didn't deserve to spend the rest of his life in prison. He wasn't going back to Raiford prison, no matter what.

Finally, he talked about the supermarket manager

being a coward for running off and leaving his employees. He praised Lois and Haralson. Then he paused, gazed hard into the camera.

"I'm going to die and go to hell tonight," he said.

Afterward, his demand satisfied, Greer appeared to lose purpose. It was like he went out of focus. He paced the tiny room, cocking and uncocking his revolver, while Lois sat at the desk trying to talk to him and Haralson stood relieved of his TV camera equipment.

For the first time during the ordeal, the policeman felt in cold fear of his own life and the life of the single remaining hostage. The bulletproof vest he wore and the hard weight of the handgun against his back underneath the vest provided little comfort. He realized he could never reach the gun in time; and he suspected Greer knew enough about bulletproof vests to shoot for the face if and when it came to that.

Yet, in spite of everything, Lord help him, Haralson yearned to keep this tormented and pitiful soul opposite him alive. They were forever joined by what they had endured together, whatever the outcome, like men who have shared a bombing raid or like survivors of a night counterattack. George Haralson had gone out of his role. He was himself, confronting himself and his life the way Greer was confronting himself, looking deep at his life in that small hot room with the convicted cop killer across from him.

He had only one more job to do. "Joe, it's all over," he said. "It's time for Lois to leave."

"No," Lois protested. "I'm not going to leave him here."

"Lois, it's time to leave," Haralson repeated, his voice stern.

Greer stopped pacing. He watched silently as the policeman pushed the woman out the door, then turned to face the convict. Haralson stood helpless, arms hanging at his sides. Greer cocked his revolver and pointed it.

"Joe, the first time you killed a policeman might have been a mistake. But I'd feel a whole lot better if you didn't have the hammer back on your gun."

Greer's inner light seemed to fade.

"Okay," he whispered.

He placed the pistol's muzzle hard underneath his own chin.

"Joe, you don't want to do this. Please. Nothing is ever solved this way."

Haralson held his breath, every nerve in his body raw.

The convict slowly uncocked the gun. It lowered. He cocked it again. The muscles in Haralson's body tightened against the expected impact of the bullet. He looked down the barrel.

This is it. He's going to kill me.

It was almost like Greer couldn't help himself, as if all the violence he had committed in his life was really inner-directed. The gun took on a life of its own. Greer couldn't have stopped it, no matter what. It turned quickly, before either man could move, and Joe Greer, cop killer, escaped convict, purged himself with a bullet through the heart. Haralson watched him do it.

Greer looked startled. Then he toppled slowly backward. His leg muscles were still twitching against the floor when SOT reacted to the gunshot, rushing into the room behind Lieutenant Thompson. Choking for air, Haralson bowled his way through the jam of uniforms all trying to get into the room at the same time.

No one noticed him now that it was over and the only death was that of the convict, who deserved it. Haralson stumbled alone into the supermarket, like the band had marched on by and left him in its wake. He made his way blindly to the deli section, fighting back bitter tears. He found an ice machine and stuck his head into the opening and grabbed great handfuls of ice and crushed them to his burning face.

Greer had killed himself while looking directly into Haralson's eyes.

When Haralson pulled his head out of the ice machine and looked up, Major Mark Andrus was standing there.

"It's over with, George," he said gently. "You did your job."

Afterword

Although the United States fields more police officers per capita than any other nation in the world, it still finds itself a very violent nation. Television news is dramatized with film showing cargo holds full of seized cocaine, police stations full of contraband weapons, handcuffed criminals being hustled into police cars, and corpses sprawled in the streets.

"Violence," said the 1960s radical H. Rap Brown, "is as American as apple pie."

And it is.

Cops are instructed to go into the streets to "prevent crime, protect life and property, arrest law violators, assist the public, preserve the public peace, regulate public conduct, and control and expedite the flow of traffic."

In doing this job, police officers bear constant witness to the dark underside of American life where violence is indeed "as American as apple pie." While most people expect relative security in the advancement of their careers, the police officer knows that the stakes in his career are much greater—his own life and the lives of others who might attempt to take it. His career and his life could end abruptly in an explosion of gunfire at the next corner, the next time he climbs rickety stairs to a junkies' pad, with the next traffic violator he pulls over.

The streets are a combat zone to the American police officer. The war against crime is a *real* shooting war, a war that continues twenty-four hours a day, day after day, year after year. In this war the cop may be called upon to sacrifice his own life—or he may be called upon to use ultimate power to preserve it or the life of another.

Cops call that power Deadly Force. Sometimes, they have no choice but to *Shoot to Kill*.